P9-CFJ-903

Other Fundraising Titles from Jossey-Bass

Made Possible By

Made Possible By

Succeeding with Sponsorship

Patricia Martin

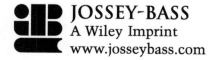

JOSSEY-BASS
A Wiley Imprint
www.josseybass.com

Published by Jossey-Bass
A Wiley Imprint
989 Market Street, San Francisco, CA 94103-1741   www.josseybass.com

Jossey-Bass books and products are available through most bookstores. To contact Jossey-Bass directly call our Customer Care Department within the U.S. at 800-956-7739 or outside the U.S. at 317-572-3986, or fax to 317-572-4002.

Jossey-Bass also publishes its books in a variety of electronic formats. Some content that appears in print may not be available in electronic books.

The publisher and the author make no representations or warranties with respect to the accuracy or completeness of the contents of this work and specifically disclaim all warranties, including without limitation warranties of fitness for a particular purpose. No warranty may be created or extended by sales or promotional materials. The advice and strategies contained herein may not be suitable for every situation. This work is sold with the understanding that the publisher is not engaged in rendering legal, accounting, or other professional services. If professional assistance is required, the services of a competent professional person should be sought. Neither the publisher nor the author shall be liable for damages arising herefrom. The fact that an organization or Web site is referred to in this work as a citation and/or a potential source of further information does not mean that the author or the publisher endorses the information the organization or Web site may provide or recommendations it may make. Further, readers should be aware that Internet Web sites listed in this work may have changed or disappeared between when this work was written and when it is read.

The ALA proposal in Chapter Four is reprinted by permission of the American Library Association.

Library of Congress Cataloging-in-Publication Data

Martin, Patricia, date.
  Made possible by : succeeding with sponsorship / Patricia Martin.—
1st ed.
    p. cm.
Includes bibliographical references and index.
  ISBN 0-7879-6502-2 (alk. paper)
  1. Corporate sponsorship. 2. Fund raising—Management.
3. Marketing—Management. I. Title.
  HD59.35.M37 2004
  658.15'224—dc22

                                                              2003021851

Printed in the United States of America

FIRST EDITION

PB Printing   10 9 8 7 6 5 4 3 2

Contents

Exhibits and Worksheets ix

Preface xi

The Author xvii

PART 1 UNDERSTANDING SPONSORSHIP

1 Making the Transition to Sponsorship 3

2 Preparing for Sponsorship 14

3 Structuring Your Offer 31

PART 2 ENGAGING WITH SPONSORS

4 Drafting the Proposal 51

5 Gaining Access to Sponsors 63

6 Selling, Negotiating, and Closing the Deal 70

7 Understanding Sponsorship's Legal and Tax Concerns 86

8 Delivering the Deal and Communicating the Results 100

Glossary 115

References 133

Index 135

1/2 210

Exhibits and Worksheets

EXHIBITS

2.1 Sponsorship Policies 22

3.1 A Marketing Plan for the Ceres Collegiate Foundation's
Women's Cardiac Care Initiative 34

3.2 Assessment Scoring Example 43

3.3 Additional Pricing Factors 44

3.4 Value Estimation Example 47

4.1 Sample Offer Letter 55

4.2 Sample Key Selling Points 58

4.3 Sample Fact Sheet 59

4.4 Sample Summary of Rights and Benefits 61

4.5 Sample Response Device 62

5.1 Sample Milestones and Timeline for Sponsorship Effort 69

6.1 Step-by-Step Sponsorship Deal Flow 71

7.1 Sample Memorandum of Intent 95

7.2 Sample Sponsorship Agreement 96

WORKSHEETS

2.1 Major Assets Your Organization Offers a Sponsor 26

2.2 Additional Assets Your Organization Offers a Sponsor 28

2.3 Media Assets Your Organization Offers a Sponsor 29

2.4 Fulfillment Capabilities Your Organization Offers a Sponsor 30

3.1 Analysis of Competitors 40

3.2 Assessing Intangibles 41

3.3 Value Estimation Formula 46

8.1 Minute Minder 101

8.2 What It Will Take to Deliver on the Agreement 103

To Emmet, Grace, and Patrick

Preface

THE CITY ZOO has a new exotic bird exhibit and an attractive entry display tells visitors a local bank helped sponsor it; a major food manufacturer donates a portion of the cost of each item shoppers purchase to a national school program; the symphony season would be a lot shorter if it weren't for the generous support of the insurance company whose name appears prominently on the program—creative *sponsorship* arrangements like these are giving many nonprofit organizations a vital boost toward achieving their missions and at the same time supplying businesses with focused access to desirable customers.

This book is part sponsorship tool-kit, part propaganda. I am telling you that upfront because it is impossible for me to disguise my fervor for sponsorship. If your nonprofit organization does not already have one or more sponsors and a process to bring more onboard, I want to recruit you to the business of identifying the sponsors who are right for you, holding discussions with their decision makers, and coming to agreement on practical and creative sponsorship deals. If your organization is already a *sponsee,* I want to help you be more competitive in the value you can offer a sponsor.

Made Possible By is a practical guide; it offers you tools and techniques I have developed and used over many years. I joined the sponsorship industry when it was still emerging, when there were no nonprofit executives whose work was dedicated solely to seeking sponsorships and I was competing with NASCAR and NFL representatives for corporations' sponsorship dollars. This book is the book I could have used then to save myself time (and occasionally embarrassment).

Every tool and technique in this book has been used to forge real alliances between for-profit and nonprofit organizations. Sponsorship took root first in sports television, in which seasoned marketing executives were both the buyers and sellers. Their sponsorship practices reflected that expertise and that environment. In an effort to be helpful, some sponsorship experts have tried to shoehorn these sophisticated, for-profit marketing methods into the nonprofit culture. This has been both helpful and harmful. It has taught nonprofit managers a great deal about how commercial marketing works, but it has also led them to believe it is easy to get their organizations to think and behave like for-profit marketers, at least when it comes to making sponsorship deals. It is, however, not easy. Too often the person leading the charge for sponsorship ends up feeling bewildered and somewhat exposed because he or she knows enough to play the game but not enough to win it.

This book offers concrete tools and approaches that have been tried by nonprofits themselves and found to get results. I also include stories and examples from the sponsors and sponsees I have encountered over the years who were either beacons of light or walking cautionary tales for what not to do. I include them both because we learn from stories of failure as much as success. Sharing the ups and downs is meant to shorten your learning cycle. For the success stories, I used people's real names. In the cautionary tales, the names of some of the organizations and individuals have been changed, and in some cases the examples are composites based on actual situations.

Made Possible By is intended for people who work in nonprofits of all descriptions. It will be relevant to large national organizations, which may have people dedicated solely to seeking sponsorship, and to the mid-sized and regional organizations that are building programs from scratch.

If you are new to sponsorship, reading this book will give you a dose of reality about what it takes. That may make you wonder if you should proceed. You may feel you are already too busy. You may wonder if sponsorship can really do anything for your organization that other revenue sources cannot. I am convinced that sponsorship will make a positive improvement in the way your organization does business, not to mention how you see yourself and your own career. Having coached several nonprofit executives as they entered the sponsorship game, I have seen firsthand the personal as well as organizational growth that can occur. Here is what to expect from mastering the process of crafting well-built sponsorship arrangements:

- You will find yourself taking a fresh look at your organization. Preparing your organization to begin a sponsorship program or to upgrade its existing effort will require you to gather information, study the community, and pull together internal team members to assess the organization's value. This work is invigorating, not a burden. You will be inspired by what you learn, and that inspiration will spread to others.

- You will become a better marketer. You will pay more attention to the way your organization engages its audiences and to the way the rest of the world markets to them as well. You will crave insight that makes you more articulate about your cause.

- You will make your organization more visible and more credible. The more promotion you do, the more opportunities you create. Signing up sponsors will elevate your organization's prestige and, more important, will generate more media images, or impressions, about your organization, raising its profile in its community.

- You will improve your organization's traditional fundraising efforts. Sponsorship is outreach. Among your sponsors will be the occasional one who finds your organization intriguing enough to join your board. Other companies will follow that lead. Your events will grow more animated with the aid of sponsor-related activities. Consider The Museum of Contemporary Art in Chicago, for example. A sponsor's commitment to lighting, music, and product showcases that are themselves artful has transformed the museum's First Friday events into extravaganzas that help convert thirty-somethings into museum members and eventually into donors.

- You will improve your ability to sell, negotiate, and close deals. No matter where you go and what career changes you make, this skill will be valuable. A good dealmaker is always in demand.

- You will establish a positive revenue stream for your organization that has fewer strings attached than foundation dollars do. A foundation typically seeks to fund a specific project; it is unlikely to be interested in providing simple operating support. Conversely, sponsorship fees are unrestricted. The sponsor pays for a package of rights and benefits. You fulfill that package. When you get the check, you spend it on your priority needs, as you see fit.

How to Use This Book

Made Possible By consists of two parts. Part One provides insights into the sponsor's rationale for investing in a nonprofit's programs and events and encourages you to complete an assessment of your organization's potential to structure a sponsorship offering that will answer a sponsor's marketing needs. The three chapters in this section help you assess what it will take to get into the game and win. Tools, examples, and worksheets will help you take the early steps necessary to build a quality sponsorship program.

Part Two deals with the practical aspects of sponsorship seeking. It covers developing a proposal, prospecting for a sponsor, and "pitching" a proposal to a sponsor. It also addresses managing relationships with sponsors once you have them, from understanding legal and tax issues to fulfilling sponsor expectations. Information, samples, tools, and case studies guide you through the process step-by-step, helping you do the work of sponsorship seeking and fulfilling. I invite you to borrow and modify the materials as you see fit. Use them to cut through the confusion and clarify

- How to handle cold calls

- How to word an offer letter

- How to craft a powerful proposal

- How to handle your first meeting with a sponsor

- How to secure your investment of time and talent by understanding the relevant legal and tax considerations

Whether you are using this book to begin learning about sponsorship, to extend your existing knowledge, or simply to review the fundamentals of your craft, I am confident that you will find yourself adapting the templates and samples

- When you're feeling stuck but need to push forward with a persuasive phrase or new idea

- When you need to provide the people inside your organization with specific process tools

- When your existing methods feel tired and you want new ways to sharpen your work

Basic Definitions

In the back of this book you will find a glossary of the special terms that are used in the following chapters and that you will encounter out in the field when dealing with sponsors and other colleagues. Here are a handful of terms that you'll need to get started.

Property. An organization, event, or celebrity that is sponsorable.

Sponsorship. A marketing strategy in which an individual or organization (the sponsor) invests cash, goods, or services in another organization or some aspect of that organization (the property) to gain access to specific assets (such as organization members or impressions) that are expected to improve the sponsor's marketplace position.

Sponsor. A person or entity that exchanges cash or in-kind goods and services for access to specific rights and benefits of a property for commercial purposes.

Sponsee. The beneficiary of the sponsor's investment.

Cause marketing. A type sponsorship whereby the sponsor creates and promotes its relationship with a charity, cause, or influential nonprofit to stimulate the purchase of products that triggers a percentage donation to be made back to the cause.

Deal. The sponsorship offer (most commonly used for an offer that has been accepted).

Sale. The presenting, negotiating, and completing of a sponsorship transaction.

Strategic philanthropy. The term used to describe corporate foundation giving programs aimed at improving the company's reputation, profile, and relationship with its customers.

Hybrid deals. Those deals that have philanthropic gifts or grants as part of the investment mix, with marketing dollars added to promote the resulting program the gift was intended to fund.

Acknowledgments

This book is a reflection of the extraordinary people who have taught me along the way, so that I could in turn teach others through workshops and now this book. Lesa Ukman and Paula Oyer-Berezin, of IEG, and Peter Petronio, now retired from Leo Burnett, opened the door to sponsorship, so that I could walk in and be successful. Lawyer Mary Hutchings Reed, a downright guru of sponsorship law, contributed insights on the legal issues relating to nonprofits and sponsorship. Special thanks also go to attorney Suzanne Ross McDowell, partner at the law firm Steptoe & Johnson LLP, Washington, D.C., for thoughtfully reviewing Chapter Seven and providing helpful comments. I would have been lost without attorney LaVerne Woods, who generously let me borrow from her seminal article on tax regulations and sponsorship, for which I am very grateful. No less generous was Joni Williams, partner at Kelly, Scott and Madison, who contributed the company's popular media glossary to add depth to the list of definitions in the back of this book.

Three people helped me get and stay focused, rescuing me from my own ramblings. Michele Fitzpatrick chipped in on the first outline, which gave birth to the project. My editor at Jossey-Bass, Johanna Vondeling, always got right to the point and insisted that I do the same. Scott Harris simply lent me his lake cabin, where I wrote my heart out without distraction.

I also have to thank my family for never carping about the nights and weekends I spent writing this book. They seemed delighted that I was doing it, even on days when I thought differently.

The best and most practical materials in this book have come from my experiences working with clients. My consulting firm, from the moment it opened its doors in 1995, has been blessed with ambitious clients, some from corporations and some from nonprofits. They have encouraged me to stretch, to pioneer beyond the existing boundaries of the discipline of sponsorship, each time discovering new territory and inventing relationships that delivered profound results. I am grateful to have worked with such talented people.

Elmhurst, Illinois   Patricia Martin
September 2003

The Author

PATRICIA MARTIN is president and founder of LitLamp Communications Group, a firm specializing in sponsorship and marketing alliances between nonprofit and for-profit organizations. Martin has helped influential organizations and corporations such as Reading Is Fundamental, Inc., National PTA, St. Louis Science Center, Georgetown University, American Licorice Company, Schering-Plough, Hiram Walker, Microsoft, MCI, and Unisys Corporation use marketing alliances to create competitive advantage.

Prior to founding LitLamp Communications, Martin served as vice president for development and sponsorship at the American Library Association (ALA), where she created a first-of-its-kind sponsorship-marketing program that generated $6.5 million in new revenue in its first eighteen months. While at ALA she partnered with Microsoft to develop the blueprint for Libraries Online! an initiative that Microsoft chairman Bill Gates has declared to be one of his most important legacies.

Martin lectures on the topic of sponsorship at the University of Chicago and the Lake Forest Graduate School of Management, and presents sponsorship seminars and workshops to nonprofit and business executives nationwide. She earned her B.A. degree from Michigan State University and her M.A. degree with honors from the National University of Ireland-University College Dublin.

Made Possible By

Part One

Understanding Sponsorship

THE FIRST THREE chapters of this book lay the foundation for your success by helping you think like a sponsor. Reading them will change your mindset about your organization—a transformation that every successful sponsorship seeker undergoes in order to be taken seriously by a sponsor.

In Chapter One you will learn why for-profit companies are attracted to sponsorship as a marketing vehicle and what makes sponsorship so successful with consumers.

Chapter Two presents the characteristics of a sponsor-worthy nonprofit organization and examines the planning and preparations required to build quality sponsorship programs. It also helps you put the information in Chapters One and Two to practical use with tools you can use to assess your organization's readiness to seek sponsorship and with tips and examples that clarify how to get started.

Chapter Three gets into the details of how you can use what you have learned about sponsorship and about your nonprofit's potential value to a sponsor to structure a sponsorship offer, putting a price on what your organization has to offer.

Chapter 1

Making the Transition to Sponsorship

WHEN NONPROFIT ORGANIZATIONS want to generate new revenue, they often turn to seeking sponsorship. The typical impulse is to use sponsorship to plug a budget hole or support a new project. The internal transformation this triggers is not immediately apparent. However, what many sponsees soon come to realize is that a sponsorship is a business deal, not a donation, and that working in the realm of sponsorship requires skills, attitudes, and insights very different from those important to everyday fundraising.

Sponsorship is a people business. This chapter introduces you to the motivations of the people who sponsor organizations like yours. It also uncovers the tangible and intangible qualities that make sponsorship a powerful tool for marketers. Knowing these qualities will help you understand why a sponsor will say "Yes!" to a partnership. Seeing your offering through the sponsor's prism will also help you make the transition to sponsorship more gracefully because you will know what sponsors know. This chapter begins your transformation from seeing your organization as a charitable cause that needs funding to seeing it as a valuable marketing partner. It is a transformation that many nonprofits are making. The following story illustrates the kinds of pressures and experiences that often mark the beginning of the transformation process.

Mark Janus, the new vice president for development at a free health clinic, has been asked to increase the clinic's corporate support by 50 percent. As a first step, he has set up meetings with the clinic's current corporate supporters to introduce himself. During these discussions he learns some hard truths.

The first meeting is with the manager of a manufacturing company's foundation, who glowers over her lunch plate. As Mark

3

probes the foundation's current priorities, she confesses that the company is reorganizing. Her job is on the line. It seems the foundation is now considered dead weight by company leaders, and the new marketing director thinks he can put funds once assigned to the foundation to better use and is consulting the company's legal counsel to explore appropriate uses.

Mark's next meeting, with the local bank manager, is equally discouraging. He learns that the bank is being merged with a large conglomerate headquartered in a completely different region.

Mark's third and final meeting is the most promising because the decision maker he is approaching appreciates the clinic and thinks it stabilizes health care availability in the community. He does have a major guideline for sponsees, however, and he tells Mark: "We will no longer fund causes that have a negative image. No downers. It has to offer an upbeat message, with lots of great photo opportunities for our employees. Get the health clinic to fit that criterion, and we'll talk."

Mark drives back to his office wondering how negatively clinic clients would react to something like a wheelchair parade. With six months to erase the clinic's $60,000 deficit, Mark realizes he is facing more than a challenge. He is facing a transformation. If he is going to succeed, the organization needs to transform its thinking about working with companies.

This situation is common. Lacking a step-by-step process for seeking and obtaining sponsors, development officers tend to think of sponsor decision makers as they do private foundation officers, and they try to work with these decision makers as they would work with foundation officers. This sets them up for exhausting cycles of researching and writing proposals and then tracking and trying to influence lengthy decision-making processes, cycles that culminate more often in dead-ends than in satisfactory relationships.

Three Transformation Basics

At the heart of the transformation needed to break out of these futile cycles is a fundamental shift in thinking. As Bernie Griffin (2002), development director at the 5th Avenue Theatre, explained: "I had to change the way I looked at my organization—[from] being a worthy cause, to being a marketing asset. . . . When I got serious about sponsorship, I had to learn how to make a whole different case."

A Change in Attitude Comes First

After years of training nonprofit leaders and staff in the skills needed to work with sponsors, I have concluded that having all the right tactics and tools can take you only so far. Just as important is your attitude as you stand in front of the sponsor. People who succeed in making good sponsorship deals for their organizations have two hallmarks. First, they are genuinely interested in working with a sponsor because they know the alliance will yield something of value for both of them, something neither could achieve alone. Second, they have the conviction that what they are offering is a good marketing investment. The people who attend my sponsorship boot camps are all bright and genuinely want to master the process. Nevertheless they struggle with it. Why? Because they fail to understand that from the sponsor's point of view sponsorship is a business proposition. This must become your point of view as well.

It's Not About Your Need—It's About Your Value

Sponsees are often budget driven. So are their requests. This is revealed by the most common failing among newcomers to sponsorship. They price what they are offering based on what it costs, not on its promotional value to the sponsor.

> One community organizer learned this lesson the hard way when she headed up a new playground building project. Her first few meetings with sponsors involved walking them through the budget for the playground. One of her best prospects chose the playground slide to sponsor. It was the most visible piece of equipment, which made it more valuable than the other items even though it was not the most expensive in actual cost. However, she sold it to the sponsor based on its cost rather than its value. This left her with less valuable but more expensive offerings for other sponsors, who were clearly going to be harder sells.

Understanding Why Sponsors Invest

Sponsors make investments in nonprofits because they wish to exploit the commercial opportunities associated with a specific event, cause, or organization. Sizing up the best deal requires the sponsor to consider both the *tangible* and the *intangible* assets that are being offered and that will help the sponsor sell more of its own products or services. When your organization makes an offer, you need to ensure that the offer features an appropriate mix of tangible and intangible assets, and then make the business case for the value of those assets to sponsors who can appreciate them.

Intangible Values Important to Sponsors

What sponsors find most valuable is the ability to link their brand to something their target market appreciates, to create an association between the brand and a positive experience in consumers' lives, especially their everyday lives. It is possible to create such associations using traditional advertising. But the impact of such advertising is as one dimensional as its delivery mechanism. Marketers turn to sponsorship because it offers them special assets that are important in people's lives and that sponsors can link with products and services to give them added importance in people's lives as well. Here are seven particularly important assets that nonprofits can share with sponsor.:

Commitment: The Magnetic Pull

Life is hectic and full of options. When people attend your nonprofit's event or pay a membership fee to affiliate with your organization, they are signaling their commitment. The gathering power of organizations and events provides sponsors with a shortcut to target audiences, audiences defined by the values their members have in common, not by what the sponsor's research dictates they should value. No one goes to the opera or participates in a 10K run for a charity on a whim. People who commit to these experiences are expressing a part of themselves that sponsors can link to in ways that run deeper than other forms of advertising do.

Lifestyle Validation

Our society grows increasingly complex. As it does so, the search for approval and reinforcement of the self will grow in power. "We never outgrow the need for approval and reinforcement of who we are," concludes clinical psychologist Sam Hamburg (2002). The values people hold and how they spend their time and money are expressions of the self. When sponsors make a lifestyle experience "possible," they validate the things their customers value and trigger a cycle of reciprocity in which the consumer rewards the company by purchasing its products. "We shopped for a mortgage, and we found the rates were all about the same, so we went with the bank that sponsored the marathon we run in every year," explained running enthusiast Charley Knapp (2002), "We figured, 'Hey, they support us, why not do the same?'"

Authenticity

According to Watts Wacker, futurist and author of *The 500 Year Delta,* "one of the most powerful of all emerging values is the demand for authenticity" ("Interview with Watts Wacker," 1997). When sponsors affiliate with a cause or event that has grown authentically from a communal desire to share an experience, they inspire trust and goodwill.

Interaction

Beyond banners and signage, smart sponsors dig in to become a meaningful part of whatever they are sponsoring. They offer samples of their products, display their wares, and provide participants with more to do and enjoy. For example, Noodle-Kidoodle sponsored a children's creative castle at a regional Celtic Festival, creating a fun way station for kids of exhausted parents who were there for the rugby, hammer tossing, ale, and music. Parents relaxed on the sidelines while their kids wielded foam swords or colored in family crests on paper that doubled as store coupons for 10 percent off. Playing host to the harried consumer, being tactile and practical, are not things we attribute to traditional advertising.

Emotional Experience

Often people buy products for emotional reasons. In their report "The Power of Product Integrity," K. Clark and T. Fujimoto (1990) noted that emotions motivate buyers: "What they are buying are values, feelings and end benefits, not technologies and product attributes." Nonprofits typically elicit emotional responses from their members or clients, the sponsor's targets, and these responses can spread to organizational sponsors also. With sponsorship the message is the medium, and the message is embedded in the preferences and lifestyles of the targets themselves. The emotional component gives a sponsor's brand a more durable identification in the consumer's mind. A case study I developed from interviews I conducted before and after an event illustrates this identification process.

> At a recent triathlon held at Stony Creek, Michigan, the Nissan X-Terra sport utility vehicle was the event's title sponsor. Many participants belonged to local bicycle, running, or swimming clubs, some for many years. Others were transplants from other cities where they had belonged to other biking or running clubs. Clearly, they were loyal to their clubs and their fellow members. "If a club member is up [to win] a medal, we have to stay around and cheer him on. It's all part of it. And when it's you, it feels great to have everybody cheering," explained Bruce Hayward (2002), a recent transplant from Rochester, New York. When a club relied for its existence on sponsor dollars, that kind of loyalty, that emotional commitment, was transferred across to the sponsor's products.
>
> Not surprisingly, then, X-Terra SUVs dotted the parking lot of this sponsored event. As the manager of the event for X-Terra

explained: "This is Nissan's second year with the event series. They have infiltrated the bike and running clubs and use them to get out [triathlon] registration information, scores, and to promote winners. They are really part of the scene. These athletes are proud to own an X-Terra."

Consumer Values

The research in marketing that laid the groundwork for the sponsorship revolution was done in the 1970s. It showed that marketers could benefit from aligning their brands with people's values because consumers' values influence their buying behavior. A value is a belief that a specific mode of conduct or a state of existence is personally or socially preferable. A person's lifestyle is an expression of his or her values. "Although opinions may vary and even conflict from time to time and situation to situation, values tend to be relatively enduring and have stronger effects on behavior" explained Durgee, O'Connor, and Veryzer (1996) in an article on consumer values and buying behavior.

In discussions of the role of personal values in buying behavior, the following five values are frequently ranked at the top of those that influence buying decisions:

- Good health

- Security

- Happiness

- Freedom

- Moral goodness

Suppose you are trying to get a sponsor interested in a *cause-related* marketing partnership (in which the sponsor creates and promotes its relationship with a charity, cause, or influential nonprofit to stimulate the purchase of products and for each purchase it gives a percentage donation to the cause). Think about how easy you can make it for a marketer to create messages that evoke moral goodness by tapping into your message. Consider the case of Harley Davidson and its support of the Muscular Dystrophy Association.

> In our culture, the motorcycle symbolizes freedom of the open road. When Harley Davidson surveyed its customers, it found a link between freedom and mobility. Muscular dysfunction is a barrier to mobility and to the kind of freedom symbolized by the motorcycle. When Harley Davidson made muscular dystrophy its corporate cause,

it aligned its brand with a profoundly held value and at the same time helped Harley Davidson riders achieve a sense of moral goodness.

Aspiration

Mercedes-Benz sponsors Tech Talks at COMDEX events for the technology industry because it wants to appeal to new economy aspirants who are hoping to acquire the trappings of traditional business success. Brands that require the buyer to pay more or to adopt an uncommon feature or new technology often sponsor organizations that offer them a connection to aspirational events and experiences. If you have a property that is prestigious and attracts a select audience, you may be able sell sponsors on supporting it in return for the aspirational appeal they will achieve when they promote their ties to your organization.

Turning These Intangibles into Gold

How can you turn these intangibles into sponsor fees? Sponsors respond to arguments that show how they can use these and other intangibles to achieve their goals. If you can discuss your organization's sponsorship value in terms of people's emotional connection to your organization's cause or offering and if you can present tactics sponsors can use to share in the loyalty, passion, or aspiration your organization inspires, you will make profound headway toward getting a deal. (In Part Two, I offer specific examples of ways to phrase your arguments.)

Tangible Values Important to Sponsors

In addition to the intangible qualities your organization can offer a sponsor, it has a number of tangible, bottom-line benefits that are attractive to sponsors. These benefits may be either inherent in a property or may arise from something attracted by the property, such as media interest that results in positive public relations.

Visibility

A newsworthy event or affiliation can yield media coverage worth many thousands of dollars, at a fraction of the cost of advertising. For corporations looking to enhance their reputation or attract influential customers, unpaid media coverage is an exceptional value. Public relations exposure typically costs 10 percent of what straight advertising costs and has the additional intangible benefit of linking the sponsor with the values associated with the nonprofit.

Efficiency

The era of the mass audience is passing. Few brands can afford to advertise their goods and services to all markets indiscriminately. Instead, companies are zeroing in and tailoring specific messages to smaller audience segments. Sponsorship is an effective vehicle for reaching audiences grouped by age, income, gender, or geography, or by psychographic characteristics.

Motivation of Retailers

Many nonprofits fail to understand the best kind of sponsorship deals to offer retailers. They go to the retailer looking for a cash deal. But the fact is that retailers have limited budgets for marketing and are in the habit of having manufacturers bring them fully developed promotions for free. The retailer wants to bring people into the store. The profits of the manufacturers and distributors of packaged goods rise and fall depending on store shelf space and position, which is controlled by store managers. Therefore they entice retailers to expand their product positioning and shelf space with product promotions and sponsorships that help drive traffic into the store. The arrangement of the wall of cereal in the average grocery store, for example, is the result of heavy manufacturer and distributor promotion and perks to retailers. Some breakfast cereal brands sponsor stock cars, but they don't do so to reach consumers directly. They make themselves visible in that sport primarily because the people who control shelf space are big stock car racing fans. In addition to sponsoring NASCAR, they provide benefits to retailers such as driver appearances at stores or complimentary tickets in exchange for additional case orders and in-store displays.

Children's Miracle Network is one of the national organizations that understands how to use the power of the retailer environment. It signed up retailer chains to carry cause marketing promotions before it approached manufacturers. Once the retailers were onboard, getting manufacturers to pay cash fees to Children's Miracle Network in return for the right to participate was much easier. Regional programs can achieve the same end by approaching retailers as promotional partners.

> Wegmans food chain, in upstate New York, has been an official sponsor of the New York Library Association's Summer Reading Program for several years. The grocery chain promotes signing up for the Summer Reading Program in its stores, prints program messages on bags, and provides in-store celebrations for groups of children who complete the program. Wegmans has helped the library system bring product manufacturer sponsors to the table, opening the door

to cash and prizes that would have been hard for the library staff to obtain otherwise.

Valuable Insights

Sometimes your organization's most valuable asset is insight into the demographic it serves. This was the case for a senior citizens organization and for a foundation focused on women's issues.

> SeniorNet is a virtual community of senior citizens that interacts on-line, running discussion groups on such issues as second marriages, transitioning households, and financial planning. Under its sponsorship tie with SeniorNet, Quaker Oats ran a study on the heart-healthy effects of eating oatmeal. Seniors signed up to participate, ordered oatmeal kits, and kept dietary journals, all on-line. This study provided Quaker Oats with valuable insight into a target market, and it provided a story to tell to the media before, during, and after the test was complete.

> The Ms. Foundation for Women tracks girls' self-esteem and body image through a variety of studies and programs. It partnered with *Seventeen* magazine to make some of these insights public, which drew the attention of companies like Johnson & Johnson and Wyeth. The Ms. Foundation built the sharing of these insights into a formal program through which sponsors pool resources in order to fund programs aimed at girls' health, and this puts these sponsors in a position to learn leading-edge information about a consumer group that is costly and often elusive to track through more commercial research methods.

Both these organizations realized that their constituent insight has market value.

Opportunity to Showcase Products

Sponsorship can give companies excellent opportunities to showcase product benefits. IBM has remained a sponsor of the Olympics for several reasons but primarily because that event is the best international tool for showcasing IBM's technological prowess as a solutions provider. Apple has invested in product placement in major motion pictures to showcase product superiority. If your property can incorporate the use of the sponsor's product—think Polartec garments worn by the climbers in the IMAX film *Everest*—then you can make the case to sponsors that their product and message are a natural fit with your organization.

Opportunity for On-Site Sales

Properties such as festivals, fairs, athletic events, and concerts lend themselves to on-site sales. If the property involves a venue where food, beverages, and souvenirs are sold, then sponsors who manufacture those items will be highly motivated to have a presence there and obtain the right to sell. These sponsors also prefer exclusivity and are willing to pay a premium for this benefit, because they know they will recoup their costs through incremental sales. Coca-Cola, for example, achieved a heightened presence in post-elementary schools though sponsorship of school athletic programs and after-school activities in exchange for the right to place vending machines in multiple locations.

Conclusion

Once you grasp the value proposition of sponsorship, and why businesses are attracted to sponsorship as a marketing platform, your transformation is under way. Understanding how to act on your new perspective is the next step in building a revenue stream from sponsorship. But, first, it's important to know just where you are starting from so you have a honest picture of what it will take to get your program going. The following reality check can help you gauge your organization's readiness to seek sponsors and the potential of the businesspeople in your region to buy in.

Some readers will tick through this list handily. Others will realize that they have considerable work to do before they can give positive answers to these questions. But every question raised here is one you will face out in the field as you begin reaching out to sponsors. The chapters that lie ahead contain the steps to get you started with that process.

Reality Check

1. Think about your organization's reach. Do you have an established marketing effort in place so that your organization keeps in touch with its constituents through e-mail, a Web site, events, newsletters, conferences, town hall meetings, television, radio or print advertising, or parties or celebrations?

2. What do you know about your organization's demographics? Have you collected recent information on who participates and why? Where they live? How far they drive to participate? Whether they are repeat users? Whether they are young families, empty-nesters, or teens? Your demographics dictate the sponsor categories on which you should focus your efforts and the ones you shouldn't waste time and energy on.

3. Have you worked with sponsors before? Do you have any testimonials from a corporate executive about the value of your organization to its community of users? Do you feature those in press kits and other marketing materials for the organization?

4. What is the competitive environment like? Look around. Are other organizations of your organization's type and in its region getting sponsorships?

5. To gauge the effort involved in reaching sponsors and meeting face-to-face, create a list of companies headquartered in your area. What do they produce, and to whom do they sell? Are there cross-promotions you can work up that will help them sell to one of your existing sponsors or team up with an existing sponsor?

6. Are you a member of civic organizations made up of businesspeople, so that you can gain insight and entrée into the business community?

7. Is there an entrepreneurial spirit in your organization? Are new ideas welcomed, and do they receive thoughtful consideration? Have other commercial or revenue-generating initiatives been realized over the last five years?

Chapter 2

Preparing for Sponsorship

RIGHT NOW your organization may not be earning considerable cash fees from sponsors. However, it may have a few corporate relationships that you suspect could lead to sponsorships. If that is the case, there are some important steps you will want to take to organize yourself before entering into more structured sponsorship deals. The information in this chapter will help you take those steps. If your organization is already involved in sponsorship arrangements, this chapter can help you evaluate whether those deals can be improved and prepare you to make better deals in the future.

Worksheets at the end of chapter will help you gather the information that is discussed here and that you will need to communicate successfully with sponsors about your organization. They will also help you discover the data gaps you need to fill in before you can command serious fees from sponsors. After undergoing this self-assessment, you will have made strides toward building a sponsorship initiative to which sponsors will respond and which your organization can support.

Whether you are starting or expanding a sponsorship program, it's a good idea to take stock of your organization. You'll need to know how your organization's audience stacks up as a marketing partner to sponsors. You'll want to understand your current organizational climate so you can start encouraging any changes needed to get staff and volunteers wholeheartedly involved in helping the organization deliver on its promises to sponsors. You'll want go through the process of setting policies that state which assets can and cannot be offered to sponsors. Finally, you will want to assess the buyer environment to learn which companies are likely prospects to benefit from a partnership with you, and why.

Assessing Your Audience: Your Best Asset

Your organization's audience—its clients, members, contributors, and other stakeholders, including people with an interest in your organization's cause—is the most important asset it has to offer a sponsor. The main reason for a company to sponsor anything is to reach the people who determine the destiny of that sponsor's product or service. Broadly considered, your audience may contain sponsor customers, regulators, distributors, or influencers, all of whom are important to the sponsor. The following sections define the various types of people that potential sponsors are looking for in your organization's audience.

End-Users

The end-user is the customer who makes the buying decision, parts with the money, and uses the product. These people might be members of your organization, come to your events, receive your newsletters, or just feel aligned emotionally with your organization's mission. The more closely your audience matches up with the existing and prospective end-users of a sponsor's product, the more valuable your organization is to that sponsor.

> Diamond Comic Book Distributors, which presents an event called International Free Comic Book Day, undertook a detailed lifestyle study of comic book readers. It discovered that the people who read comic books frequently consume candy and snack foods just as frequently. It seems a comic book is a trigger to buy candy to eat while reading. This relationship in the data crossed over all reader age groups, regional groups, and income brackets, which meant it was a defining characteristic of the comic book audience. Equipped with this information, Diamond Comic Book Distributors could narrow the focus of its search for event sponsor prospects to a wide variety of candy and snack food manufacturers. Barry Lyga (2003), marketing director for International Free Comic Book Day explained, "I started with a long list of prospects from all sorts of companies. After looking at the research, I focused my approach. I know exactly who they are and what they want, and it is precisely what I can deliver."

People in the Business Channel

A business channel is made up of individuals who sell or resell the product or otherwise make it available for sale to the buyer. Think Avon lady, State Farm Insurance salesperson, grocery store manager, Culligan man, and Ford dealer. These are businesspeople in their own right who are licensed or trained to sell and service a product. As you take stock of your audience, consider whether you have access to any people who represent a business channel. Is there a car dealer or grocery store manager on your board, for example? Is a local retailer supporting your family events or a gala? Could that relationship represent an opportunity for another company, perhaps an apparel or home products company, that wants to improve its relationship with the people in this channel?

Distributors

Distributors control which brands make it to the shelf so consumers can buy them. They differ from channel players because they are not licensees of branded lines; their role is to deliver multiple brands to retailers. Here is how one organization used a connection with a distributor to sign up several sponsors.

> The Ravinia Music Festival partnered with a major liquor distributor to present a variety of tastings and to introduce several new wines to the concession operation at Ravinia's outdoor music venue. Jeanine LaRouche (2002), associate director of development for corporate relations at Ravinia, was new to the festival at the time but not to sponsorship. While taking stock of the organization in her first few weeks, LaRouche interviewed the festival's concession management, learned of the distributor relationship, and recognized the potential for sponsorship. After a deal was made the distributor became the conduit for marketing dollars from several brands, creating a meaningful pool of dollars. Furthermore, the distributor orchestrated participation from a grocery chain that ran a promotion offering a special discount on Ravinia tickets for its customers, which drove traffic into stores. The grocery chain bought the block of tickets it would sell at a discount, so that Ravinia was guaranteed this revenue, and it created large areas in its stores to showcase the participating wineries and promote Ravinia.

The Media

Because companies find it difficult to get the news and entertainment media to write about or show their products, they seek to capture media attention through newsworthy relationships. For instance, Olympic sponsor Sara Lee attracted media attention to a company product during the Winter Olympics held in Sarajevo when sportswriters ran out of underwear, and Sara Lee representatives distributed free Hanes underwear to them. And Bloomingdale's attracted national media attention across multiple markets when it partnered with the Broadway production of the musical *Hairspray*. Ann Keating (2002), PR director for Bloomingdale's led the relationship, offering a themed *Hairspray* section in the store along with multiple copromotions designed to circulate traffic between the production and the store.

Many nonprofits enjoy a warm relationship with the media. Ask yourself whether you find it easy to get stories written about your organization. Socially relevant or highly visual causes and events often command impressive power with the media that sponsors can borrow. Zoos, outdoor concerts, and parades that have visual interest also fall into this category. As Wayne Retherford, executive director of the Illinois St. Andrew Society, which hosts the annual Chicago Highland Games, puts it, "When the press calls to schedule their photographer, they want to know when the men will throw the big objects." The sport of caber tossing is not something you see everyday, so it's news. While working with Retherford, my firm encouraged him to place his sponsor's signage near the site of this event and to set up the media area so that the sponsor's signage would be captured in most press shots.

It's easy to gauge your organization's newsworthiness. Start gathering evidence of media interest: lists of the media that have done stories about or mentioned your organization (TV, radio, newspapers and other publications), with the dates on which the items appeared, and copies of clippings and, when possible, videocassettes can prove your organization can deliver the media as an audience type.

Civic Leaders and Industry Regulators

For highly regulated industries such as petroleum and telecommunications reaching members of the U.S. Congress is a must. State and city officials and members of groups involved in community action are also an important audience for many businesses. Sponsorship may be important to companies with products and services that have fallen under scrutiny by legislators or concerned citizens. For instance, when the "cola wars" spilled over into schools, Coca-Cola and Pepsi waged bitter battles to secure an exclusive presence in school districts. The recent backlash from parents has led to discussions among civic leaders about eliminating carbonated beverages from schools entirely, on nutritional grounds. Coke and Pepsi are now sponsoring educational and youth development causes to improve their image among civic leaders and education officials.

Measuring Your Audience

Prospective sponsors will evaluate the quality of your organization's audience. In addition to looking at the kinds of people your organization attracts, they will be looking at audience numbers and geographical distribution and at whether your audience has some elite status. It is my experience that an organization's ability to do a thorough and accurate job of measuring and communicating information about its audience makes it easier for a sponsor to make the decision to invest. As you assess your organization's readiness to go to market with sponsorship offerings, gather up all the data you can about your audience, and create a plan for filling in the information you don't currently know by doing some research.

Having accurate information on the following audience characteristics will significantly strengthen your case with sponsors.

- Audience size
- Geographical distribution
- Household incomes
- Education levels
- Business titles
- Marital status
- Number of children living at home
- Gender
- How far they travel to attend your event
- How frequently they attend
- Consuming habits

    How often do they travel—for leisure and for business?

    How old is the vehicle they drive?

    How often do they dine out?

    Do they purchase beer, wine, or spirits?

    Do they use the Internet to shop?

    What magazines do they read?

You may decide to hire a professional market researcher to help you gather information about your organization's audience. This can be a great investment. The professional knows what to ask and how to ask it to yield the most compelling data. Consider also that third-party research and assessment is always more credible to a sponsor than in-house research.

Evaluating Your Organization's Culture: Is It Ready for Sponsorship?

Some of what it takes to succeed at sponsorship is pure common sense—be visible, reach out, return phone calls, act professionally, and deliver on your promises. But in the quest to get out there and make deals happen, it is very easy to lose track of some simple realities. One of these realities is that you represent an organization that is a complex system of people who have their own responsibilities and agendas. No matter how talented you are, you will need others in your organization to help you deliver what you promise to the sponsor. To get a feel for your organization's readiness to get behind a serious sponsorship program, consider your nonprofit in light of the following attributes of organizations that succeed in attracting and maintaining sponsorship arrangements.

Ten Attributes of Nonprofits That Are Sponsorship Powerhouses

1. Their culture is entrepreneurial. It allows for risk taking and sets benchmarks for achieving financial goals in new ventures.

2. They are flexible. They quickly assemble effective, cross-functional teams around tasks. These teams run efficient meetings to solve problems and report information. Roles and goals are quickly established and reinforced. When the task is completed, the group dissolves if it needs to, without turf issues.

3. They offer superior events and programs. In a recent interview with Sandi Reitelman (2002), former marketing manager of the Brooklyn Academy of Music (BAM), I asked her to explain BAM's success, given its out-of-the-way location and the amount of competition in New York City. "Programming is everything," she explained, "Nothing builds an audience like programs people feel they must see."

4. They have a clear understanding that sponsorship is an exchange of fees for marketing assets, not a fundraising tool to pay the cost of a project or answer a budget shortfall. You can spot whether or not an organization has this understanding by doing the math. For example, when the head of regional museum called me to ask if I could recommend a good sponsor prospect for a touring exhibit he was planning, I asked a few pertinent questions about the media exposure expected and the number of markets on the tour. Then I asked the price point for the top-tier package. The museum head said, "Well, the whole thing is costing us $1 million to build." But judging from the other information he had shared, there wasn't a million dollars worth of promotional

value in the package. He was fundraising for a project, not selling a sponsorship deal.

5. They know their audience. These organizations possess detailed, up-to-date intelligence on their audience, acquired through a variety of instruments and reference points.

6. They do aggressive outreach. These nonprofits value communication and do it very well, even on tight budgets. Marj Halpern (2002), executive director of the League of Chicago Theatres, is one of the pluckiest marketers I know. During the economic downturn that followed September 11, 2001, the League's cash sponsors closed their checkbooks. Undaunted, she pulled together restaurants, hotels, and luxury shops to sponsor special promotions for value-priced packages involving theater evenings and "get away someplace close" weekend packages. No cash changed hands, but in addition to free promotion, she asked for in-kind support in the form of free hotel rooms and free dinner coupons to distribute to the League's member theaters to use for their own promotions or to relieve their budgets. With zero dollars she kept live theater a hot ticket in tough times.

7. They have leaders and staff who enjoy regular contact with business-people. These organizations interact with businesspeople in a variety of ways, not solely to seek revenue. The person charged with finding sponsors belongs to business organizations and regularly attends business-to-business events in the community.

8. They are responsive. They keep sales materials ready to go in order to keep communications flowing between themselves and their prospects.

9. They set realistic sales goals. They know it takes time to build a sponsorship program, and they plot their timelines and project revenues accordingly.

10. They can deliver what they promise. They have written policies to guide their negotiations, and they have buy-in across the organization to support the sponsorship effort with action.

Creating Sponsorship Policies

In light of today's business climate, it's a good idea to have written policies in place that clarify what can and cannot be done when working with sponsors. The policies need not be lengthy or all encompassing. Assume that you'll need to review them occasionally, and feel free to make adjustments for situations that seem to recur. Doing the spadework of policy setting early pays off later when you are in the heat of deal making. You don't want to be forced to halt the flow of negotiations because you have to tackle weighty issues back at your organization. Lapses in alacrity can kill a deal. Although it is impossible to imagine and prepare for all the issues you may confront, the thinking ahead you can do often pays off. Here are a few of the questions that commonly crop up in negotiations and that you should be prepared to answer promptly:

- Will the sponsor be permitted to use your organization's logo on its materials or packaging?

- Will your organization make its database of members and donors available to the sponsor and under what restrictions? (Printed labels? One-time use? Universal access?)

- Will your organization provide an official endorsement of the sponsor's product or service?

- Will your organization collaborate on program or event content?

- Are there business categories that are off limits to your organization? (For example, nonprofits may determine that they will not sponsor with companies involved with firearms, tobacco, or spirits.)

- Are there product or service standards the sponsor must meet? (You can research such standards through consumer guides and consumer watchdog organizations.)

One of the best ways to set sponsorship policies is to convene a corporate relations committee to review the issues. The committee chair leads the group through some what-if scenarios and gets group members' consensus on what the organization's stance should be in each case. Once initial policies have been agreed on, write them down, and circulate them. Call these written versions "working documents" in order to leave room in people's minds for a policy refinement process once the organization has a few deals under its belt.

Written policies tend to vary according to the nonprofit type. The policies for a health-related charity or a children's charity, for instance, will be different from those for a symphony orchestra. To give you an idea of what a nonprofit's written policies might look like, however, Exhibit 2.1 shows a generic policy document (created for a hypothetical organization).

EXHIBIT 2.1

Sponsorship Policies

The National Parents for a Better Way Association applies the following policies when partnering with corporations:

1. Before any proposals can be developed or significant information can be divulged regarding our programs beyond our public brochures, we must know the identity of the prospective sponsor.

2. Access to our membership will be carefully controlled through mailings handled by us. We will not release the names of individuals who are members or donors for use by a sponsor.

3. Children's photos or creative work cannot be used without signed release forms, and all artwork, use of our name, or copy treatments developed as a result of any partnership must be preapproved by us.

4. We will not allow our name, marks, and/or logo to be used in relation to an official endorsement of a sponsor's product or company.

5. We will not partner with tobacco, alcohol, or firearms companies, or with companies' media outlets that promote messages that seem contrary to our stated mission.

6. Sponsors who provide in-kind support will be reviewed on a case-by-case basis to judge whether fair market value can be assessed and a mutually beneficial partnership can be achieved.

7. We will make our best efforts to accommodate sponsors who want to combine philanthropic gifts with sponsorships, and we will keep good records of our transactions to fulfill our reporting obligations to the IRS.

8. Corporate partnerships will not be a financial hardship for us. Expenses to implement any partnership must be accounted for, and should not exceed any fees paid to us by the sponsor.

9. Anytime a sponsor wishes to codevelop program materials for use by our constituents, our editorial guidelines must be followed.

10. All sponsorships will be based on a written agreement.

11. All sponsorship opportunities and negotiations must be coordinated through our chief development officer in charge of corporate relations.

Sizing Up the Sponsor Market

Your initial assessment has to include a review of the corporate community to identify businesses that will be interested in your audience and your offer. The business categories discussed here are not meant to be exhaustive, but they are broadly representative of the types of businesses that are active in sponsorship at local, regional, and national levels.

Corporate Headquarters

If you are approaching a company that is headquartered in your city, the sponsor will have a vested interest in the quality of life in your community. Its employees appreciate lifestyle amenities and social services that make the region a better home for themselves and their families. Hometown sponsors will pay more for a relationship. Their motives for supporting non-profits are often a blend of philanthropy and sponsorship, which means they are interested in building reputation as well as getting value from your assets. So any public relations efforts you can offer will matter almost as much to them as having their names featured in paid media. To appeal to a hometown sponsor, be prepared to demonstrate your organization's contribution to the community's quality of life.

Media Companies

Media sponsors can play one of two roles: they can pay a sponsorship fee for a property in cash and then negotiate the right to resell that property to their advertisers (along with beefed-up advertising packages), or they can provide promotional consideration (airtime or print space). Cash fees are less likely than promotional consideration. The big issue for media companies is the ability to sell more than just sponsee-linked airtime or print space to their own advertisers. Print, radio, and TV sponsors often engage in sponsorship to receive benefits such as the right to offer on-site sampling and hospitality to the audience at the nonprofit's events and venues, so they can in turn sell these rights to their advertisers, thus offering these advertisers a value-added package.

To attract media sponsors then, nonprofits must provide publishers and radio and TV outlets with ways to involve their advertisers in the event.

Beverage Companies

Beverage companies look for two things in a sponsorship arrangement: the right imagery to associate with their brand and the opportunity to sell their product at sponsee venues. If your organization also has a relationship with a grocery retailer, the latter opportunity will matter less if you can construct a three-way partnership, as I described in the case of the Ravinia Music Festival earlier in this chapter. Because beverage companies are in a very competitive industry and their profit margins are razor thin, attracting a beverage sponsor solely with the opportunity to link with your organization's image will be difficult.

Financial Services Companies

Take a grassroots approach to financial services companies. All sales in banking, investment, and insurance services happen locally. Typically, local offices are small, they sell to local people, and they rely on the national headquarters to dream up promotions that are turnkey (that is, completely ready to roll).

I once managed a sponsorship deal between a nonprofit and a major insurance agency. They collaborated on a consumer-focused college savings program that included a national sweepstakes to win college tuition. Local agents received a newsletter discussing how to finance college tuition to distribute to customers. And parents could sign up to receive a more substantial guidebook, which generated a database of parent names. Agents had the option of hand delivering these guidebooks to the families who requested them, so they could make personal contact and build rapport.

Financial services companies also look for generous, free-ticket packages for local agents who participate in a sponsorship program. When working with this type of business, consider incorporating a "door-opener" package that folds in assets such as a golf outing, reception, or similar event where company agents can meet potential clients. This gives them a much-needed entrée to their target market in a relevant, local setting.

Banks especially look for grassroots ties that also deliver big visibility. Invite a banking sponsor to work its sponsorship involvement for the benefit of both its consumer banking and its business banking. Emphasize a hospitality package (a sponsored event for the sponsor's clients) for its business banking division. Offer to work together with the sponsor on event seating to ensure that the sponsors' people are seated next to potential clients. Banks like event signage, especially when their identities are shifting owing to mergers and they need to publicize a new name.

Telecommunications Companies

Telecommunications was once a red-hot business category in sponsorship. But through consolidation of firms and the problems of major companies such as MCI WorldCom and Lucent, this sector has cooled. However, regional telecoms and national wireless companies are still active, and major telecoms' need for local relevance is still driving their money into regional sponsorships. These sponsors don't need to be convinced that sponsorship works, they were early adopters. They just need evidence that they can achieve certain objectives such as building a database of potential customers, having opportunities to offer promotions, and creating consumer loyalty for a notoriously price-based commodity.

Retail Companies

Retailers have enormous power in that, as discussed in Chapter One, they control shelf space and positioning on the sales floor. An end-of-the-aisle display of special-price items can literally double sales for the length of the promotion. However, retailers also have limited budgets and prefer to get manufacturers to help them pay for a promotion. They can deliver the manufacturers who contribute cash support to you in return for shelf space and promotional consideration including coupons, shelf-talkers (small signs placed at the point of sale in retail to attract the eye and convey a promotional message), and ads in weekly in-store flyers, all linked to your organization.

Apparel Companies

Acquiring an apparel sponsor, or for that matter any product sponsor who relies on a retail channel, means that you have to think about how you can help the sponsor work with a retail partner who carries a themed in-store promotion to drive sales (again, the Ravinia case is a relevant example).

Automotive Companies

A car is a carefully considered purchase. People will take months shopping for the right vehicle. For this reason, finding ways to stimulate the intent to buy is everything for automobile manufacturers and dealers. Detroit wisdom holds that it takes consumers seven to ten interactions with a vehicle—seeing, touching, and test-driving—to inspire them to buy. So any approach to an automotive company must address means of displaying vehicles, signing people up for test-drives, and building traffic into dealerships. Car companies vary in their approaches to managing sponsorship dollars, but most have national marketing funds and regional funds, and local dealerships have discretionary dollars. Local dealers prefer to spend these dollars on traditional advertising. If yours is a regional property, approach the automaker's regional marketing office first and add the national director to your mailing list to make him or her aware of your program. Local dealerships may also be targets if they are savvy and willing to think beyond traditional advertising.

Tools for Self-Assessment

Now complete the following four worksheets, involving others in your organization as appropriate. This will help you identify your organization's strengths as a sponsee and the areas in which it needs to acquire more data or perhaps consider making some changes. In general, these worksheets address things sponsors want to know about a sponsorable property regardless of their own business category. Of course, sponsors will also be evaluating your property with an eye to the type of business they are in and the kind of sales impact they hope to achieve.

WORKSHEET 2.1

Major Assets Your Organization Offers a Sponsor

Answer the questions on this worksheet to the best of your ability. (You may have to conduct further research before you can answer all the questions.) This will prepare you to give guidance to a sponsor for determining the value of three critical assets: your geographical reach, the time periods in which your organization would fulfill sponsor promotions, and the demographics of your audience.

Location and Promotional Timeframe

1. Is your organization represented in the five largest U.S. markets (as determined by the A. C. Nielsen Company)? Check off the markets in which your organization is represented.

   ☐ New York

   ☐ Los Angeles

   ☐ Chicago

   ☐ Philadelphia

   ☐ San Francisco–Oakland

2. In the space below, list the geographical markets where your organization has the most influence (these markets might be specific neighborhoods, towns, cities, counties, and so on).

   _____

   _____

   _____

   _____

   _____

3. Many sponsor promotions are time sensitive. Please check off the periods in which your organization holds its events or could make other assets available to sponsors. (The year-round category typically has more value to sponsors.) If quarters are not appropriate for the sponsors you are considering, change the categories as necessary.

   ☐ First quarter—winter

   ☐ Second quarter—spring

   ☐ Third quarter—summer

   ☐ Fourth quarter—fall

   ☐ Year-round

WORKSHEET 2.1, Cont'd

Audience Demographics

1. What is the total number of people in your organization's audience (for example, attendance, membership, affiliates, and so forth)?

   _____ People in audience

2. What is the total number of names on your organization's mailing list?

   _____ Mailing list names

3. What is the age range of the people in your organization's audience? (The value of each age group will depend on the sponsor's objectives, but adults 21 to 45 years old tend to be desired by many sponsors.) Check all the categories that apply. If you know the percentages for each age range, please supply them.

   ☐ Children and youth

   ☐ Adults (21–35)

   ☐ Adults (36–45)

   ☐ Mature adults

4. What percentage of your organization's audience is male and what percentage is female?

   _____ % Male

   _____ % Female

5. Rank the following categories of household income from 1 to 3, with 1 being the category most common among your audience and 3 being the category least common among your audience. (Higher income levels typically are of more value to sponsors because they connote more purchasing power.)

   _____ $35,000 or less

   _____ $35,001–$74,999

   _____ $75,000 or more

6. Rank the following categories of education levels from 1 to 3, with 1 being the category most common and 3 being the category least common among your audience.

   _____ Completed college

   _____ Some college

   _____ High school diploma/GED

WORKSHEET 2.2

Additional Assets Your Organization Offers a Sponsor

Check the box in front of each additional benefit your organization could make available to a sponsor. This list is not exhaustive (for instance, my firm once worked with a zoo that sold sponsors' naming rights to its large mammals), so treat it as a jumping off point and let it inspire your thinking about what more your organization might offer.

Access to those affiliated with your organization or event (database or mailing list access)

☐ Use of your logo

☐ Naming rights to venue, event, or series

☐ Sponsor ID on collaterals

☐ Sponsor ID on school outreach materials

☐ Sponsor mention onstage, in printed programs, on ticket fronts, on posters, and so on

☐ Ad in printed programs

☐ On-site sponsor presence at your events for product display, product sampling, offering coupons, conducting research, selling products, signing people up for test drives or other product demonstrations

☐ Access to your volunteers for help with product sampling, disseminating materials, and so on

☐ Right to channel promotions down to your affiliate groups, chapters, or venues

☐ Sponsor exclusivity (only one company per industry is allowed to be a sponsor)

☐ Shared on-line (Web site) presence

☐ Shared advertising

☐ Sponsor employee or employee family involvement and events

☐ Sponsor-provided VIP services or hospitality for your audience

☐ Event or gala tickets for sponsor use

☐ Private receptions or VIP meet-and-greets for sponsors

☐ Right to hold corporate events at your venue

☐ Other benefits (write in below):

_____

_____

_____

_____

_____

WORKSHEET 2.3

Media Assets Your Organization Offers a Sponsor

List any media your organization owns or controls that you would make available to a sponsor or advertiser. For each item, indicate the frequency of its appearance, its circulation (or viewership or listenership), and whether it sells advertising space. (Note that the average value to the sponsor of shared advertising where the sponsor logo appears prominently in the ad is 10 percent of the ad's total cost.) Also list any special terms or conditions that apply to the use of each medium.

Medium (Print, Internet, Radio, TV)	Frequency	Circulation	Ad Space for Sale (Y or N)	Special Terms or Conditions

If ad space is available in any of these items, are rate cards available?   Yes ____   No ____

WORKSHEET 2.4

Fulfillment Capabilities Your Organization Offers a Sponsor

Does your organization have staff devoted to working with corporate sponsors? If yes, indicate the number of people available in each category listed below.

___ Yes

    ___ Full-time

    ___ Part-time

    ___ Volunteers

___ No

Conclusion

After completing the self-assessment exercises in this chapter, you will have made considerable strides toward building a sponsorship initiative that will be attractive to sponsors and embraced by your organization. In spirit, sponsorship will always be about achieving a partnership where all parties share their most robust marketing assets. The benefits you offer arise out of those assets. Even though each business will place somewhat different values on each benefit, depending on its perceived usefulness, all prospective sponsors will recognize and appreciate a sponsor-seeking nonprofit that has done its homework before its representatives ever knock on the door.

Chapter 3

Structuring Your Offer

STRUCTURING A SPONSORSHIP OFFER can be complex. My firm treats it like a science, calculating the fair market value of everything on offer, from a brochure to a handshake, using an elaborate matrix based on the hundreds of deals I track annually. Because market values shift constantly, I update the matrix quarterly. To simplify the process for your purposes, I have boiled it down to a few basic formulas, although I don't mean to minimize the complexity. The work of setting prices will always be made difficult by the way gray areas show up in the middle of calculations you would rather carry out in clear-cut, black and white terms.

My purpose in sharing this information is to help you develop a pricing strategy that fits your organization. To succeed in attracting and working with sponsors you need an objective valuation of the benefits your organization is offering each sponsor, not just your costs. Otherwise you walk into the sales process unprepared for the *exchange* that makes the deal, the exchange of the sponsor's fee for your organization's assets.

No matter how elaborate the sponsorable property, its pricing comes down to three factors:

1. What the competition (other sponsorable properties) is getting and what it is giving in return.

2. The number of people your organization reaches and the methods it uses to reach them.

3. Intangible qualities that add value.

In this chapter you will determine a price range for your offering, based on its potential value to a sponsor, not the financial need within your organization. You will learn how each of the three pricing factors applies to your offering. Completing the worksheets in this chapter will not only help you determine your pricing but will assist you in removing the emotion from the pricing process. Over the years I have helped a wide variety of clients ascertain their fair market value, and I have observed that their dedication to their organization's mission can cloud their judgment in the pricing process. The worksheets will focus you on the reality. After completing the work of this chapter, you will know the strong and weak points of your property before you encounter a sponsor. You will have an understanding of your organization's worth based on an objective assessment of its tangible and intangible marketing assets. This chapter will also help you assemble your marketing assets in a way that is strategic for your organization, by starting with a marketing plan.

Building Your Marketing Plan with Tangible Assets

You determine the tangible value of your property by focusing on your audience and the methods you use to reach them. It will not be enough to claim that you have developed a loyal audience; you must demonstrate to a potential sponsor that you reach this audience consistently and that its members participate regularly. Remember, the sponsor's objective is to communicate through your organization. Tucked into your marketing plan should be media and public relations strategies that help you and the sponsor deliver impressions to your broadest audience. These are your most tangible assets.

Once you have been through the process of preparing a marketing plan, you will

- Be able to communicate to sponsors that you are thoughtful about marketing and have strategies in place to advance your organization's cause and their partnership with it.

- Have concrete conversations with sponsors. You will bring focus to meetings and proposals because you are sharing your intentions, and sponsors will do the same, opening the door to the win-win discussions that can yield solid partnerships.

- Have a road map to share with your colleagues in your organization, making it easier for them to line up behind you.

Your organization may already have a comprehensive marketing plan. Complex organizations may have a general plan and several subplans. For instance, a museum might have one marketing plan for membership, one for exhibitions, one for school groups, and one for an annual fashion show.

If you already have one or more plans, you are in luck. If not, better still. You can use the process of creating a marketing plan to build internal support for the sponsorship initiative that will follow. You probably have a sense of who in your organization contributes to communicating with key constituent groups, and you can take these steps:

1. Select respected decision makers, people who are likely to be supportive of developing a marketing plan.

2. Go to each, and explain why you think the organization will benefit from having a formal marketing plan.

3. Ask if they have any immediate thoughts or know of any issues you should know about.

4. Discuss their involvement and what you expect of them in terms of time and input.

5. Develop a planning process.

6. Create a timetable with clear-cut milestones and expected deliverables.

7. Begin meeting together.

The following list is a tool for guiding your first few planning sessions. Modify the questions as you see fit, and use these sessions to hash out differences of opinion about how the organization should be positioning itself. (Have someone at the meetings whose job is to capture people's thoughts.)

Questions to Clarify Marketing Directions

- What are our organization's attributes (facts about the organization)?

- What audiences (both primary and secondary) do we serve?

- What do they know about us?

- What don't they know about us?

- What are the key messages we need to communicate?

- What is the desired response to these messages?

- What are we currently doing that helps us get this response?

- How much more will we need to do to achieve our expected result?

- How will we measure our success?

Converting the information you gather from the team into a marketing plan is a solo task. The team members will be worn down from wrangling about preferences for specific marketing tactics. Take their insights and begin crafting the plan. In general, when engaging groups in creative activities, it is best to move from the concrete to the abstract. You can return later with the written plan (concrete) and walk the team through it for final ideas and refinements (abstract.)

Marketing plans come in all shapes and sizes. Some are heavily detailed, right down to launch dates and treatments for printed matter. Others are outlines with bulleted highlights. Because your marketing plan may become part of your sponsor pitch, you will need more than an outline. What I call an "abbreviated marketing plan" contains a practical level of detail. Exhibit 3.1 presents an example of an abbreviated marketing plan.

EXHIBIT 3.1

A Marketing Plan for the Ceres Collegiate Foundation's Women's Cardiac Care Initiative

Situation

The Ceres Collegiate Foundation has supported women's cardiac care as its national philanthropy since 1946. Since that time, thousands of dollars have been raised by local collegiate and alumnae chapters for the cause, and the Ceres Collegiate Foundation has given grants to health care professionals and medical facilities around the country.

To create greater visibility, both within Ceres Collegiate and in the general public, the Foundation is planning a campaign that would raise visibility for its cardiac care program, and provide all chapters with resources and know-how for supporting this cause.

Goals

- Raise visibility for the Ceres Collegiate Foundation
- Increase awareness about cardiac care for women
- Position the Ceres Collegiate Foundation to stimulate:

    Ongoing sponsor investments

    Contributions from members

    National media

    New member recruitment

Cardiac Care Platform Assets and Barriers

Assets

- Over 90,000 members across the United States and Canada
- Access to desirable collegiate audience
- Built-in distribution network
- Timeliness of women's health issues
- Collegiate chapters and alumnae asking for more information about cardiac care

EXHIBIT 3.1

A Marketing Plan for the Ceres Collegiate Foundation's Women's Cardiac Care Initiative, Cont'd

Barriers

- Market for women's cardiac care information dominated by American Heart Association
- General public does not distinguish between Greek organizations
- Lack of credentials as a health organization

Marketing Aims

- Capture interest early
- Build Ceres Collegiate brand equity
- Heighten the call-to-action

Tone. Sincere, energetic, empowering.

Look. Warm yet educational.

Key Benefit to Communicate. The Ceres Collegiate Foundation is a supporter of women's cardiac care through grant money, availability of educational materials, and innovative programming for members.

Target Audience

- Alumnae and collegians
- Corporate sponsors
- Health care community
- Precollege girls
- University community

Spillover Audience

- Parents
- Young girls
- News media

Scope. National.

Campaign Overview

Timing. The women's cardiac care initiative should be announced at the next international convention, with materials ready to roll out to collegiate chapters that following fall. Host a workshop for collegiate officers and one for alumnae officers to educate them about the program and how they can participate.

We recommend that Cardiac Care Week remain in February of each year.

EXHIBIT 3.1

A Marketing Plan for the Ceres Collegiate Foundation's Women's Cardiac Care Initiative, Cont'd

Partner Involvement. Create a relationship with an association that can provide medical credibility and co-branded educational materials, like the National Heart, Lung, and Blood Institute or the American Heart Association.

National Programs. Create a specific fund for cardiac care, called "Follow Your Heart" Fund.

Create an Advisory Panel from Cardiac Care Week. The panel should include cardiac care researchers/physicians, Ceres Collegiates, partner organization members, and representatives from any corporate sponsors. The advisory panel would select the winners for the cardiac care grant money each year.

Collegiate Programs. Hold one big, attention-getting event each year. Chapters can apply for the right to host the event each year. The event has a heart-healthy twist, such as the world's largest pot of oatmeal or the world's longest breakfast table. Spotlight this activity in the Quarterly, and promote it to the national media. The local chapter will involve the Greek community as well as the university to produce this event.

All other Ceres Collegiate chapters will host one activity during Cardiac Care Week on campus that has a heart-healthy focus; i.e., walk-a-thon, 5K race, jive dance, jump-rope-a-thon, pogo sticks, oatmeal eating contest, etc. This activity should be a fundraiser for the Foundation.

Chapters should host a heart screening day on campus. At this event, names can be captured on postcards. This drives a database to which information can be sent later about healthy hearts, and also about Ceres Collegiate. At this screening, give away "quick page finders" (inserts into day planners that mark the day for you). The page finder can have the top 5 healthy heart tips and the Ceres Collegiate logo.

Alumnae Programs. Alumnae need access to educational materials. Have educational materials and the quick page finders available. Alumnae can call and order the materials, or request them on-line from the Foundation.

Coordinate a speakers network so alumnae chapters can host educational meetings. Again, this information could be made available on the Foundation section of the Ceres Collegiate Web site.

Health Care Providers. Local health care providers can be involved in local collegiate and alumnae chapters in a number of ways. It will be necessary to invite them to assist with heart screening activities on campus or at alumnae chapter meetings. Educational materials can also be distributed by collegians to local hospitals and health care centers that go on display for patients.

Campaign Collaterals

- Officer materials. Overview of campaign and new programs. Can be sent as insert to collegiate notebook—"Why We Need Each Other."
- New pages about women's cardiac care on the Ceres Collegiate Web site. Link to any partners. Recognize sponsors.
- Educational materials for members.
- Quick page finders to give away to members and nonmembers.
- Ad in *CASE Currents* announcing Professor of the Year (with women's cardiac care theme).

EXHIBIT 3.1

A Marketing Plan for the Ceres Collegiate Foundation's Women's Cardiac Care Initiative, Cont'd

Media Strategies

Overall. To deliver established objectives, a $150,000 marketing budget would be ideal to achieve a mix of public relations, special events, word-of-mouth, plus guaranteed outdoor and targeted print and radio. Sponsor paid promotions can drive further impressions.

Steps

- Unveil the campaign and announce any partners at the annual Convention.
- Craft detailed word-of-mouth campaign for each target subset.
- Leverage all existing paid and earned media to carry out the campaign.
- Seek sponsors and media partners who can provide cash and/or media inventory to the campaign.
- Drive messages and unpaid media by unveiling the campaign in waves to stimulate curiosity, build leadership, and generate word-of-mouth.

Sizing Up the Competition

Establishing a fair market price for the assets your organization has to offer is somewhat similar to the process a realtor goes through when setting the price for a house. The realtor researches comparable properties that have been sold in the area to find out what buyers paid for them. Even though each home has unique attributes and beauty is in the eye of the beholder, there are standard features that can be compared, such as the number of bedrooms, the lot size, the kind of garage provided, and so on. Similarly, a critical piece of your pricing puzzle is to uncover what sponsors have paid for comparable marketing opportunities.

Doing a competitive analysis requires some detective work. Look around. What are all the possible places and vehicles that the companies on your prospect list can use to reach their target audience? The answer to that question represents your competition. When sponsors size up your offer, they will compare your price and deliverables against the price and deliverables offered by other media and outreach vehicles in your marketplace. Do your research to uncover how those vehicles are priced and what they deliver, as this theater producer did.

> Michael Miller is the producer, and also an actor, for a small theater company in an ethnically diverse neighborhood in Chicago. The theater has a small but loyal audience base that subscribes to series

tickets, pays additional money to park, and is willing to venture into the neighborhood for evening performances. Still, when Michael was seeking a sponsor, he was realistic. He knew he could not attract the likes of Sara Lee or Jaguar International with his small audience. Instead, he looked around at the other businesses in his neighborhood that were also thriving during evening hours and that might be sponsor prospects and began keeping a log of where and how they were advertising. The local bank had signage at bus stops. A café advertised in the local newspaper, as did the local car dealership. The gourmet pizza shop had signage at the bowling alley and ran coupons in church newsletters. He contacted all of these media outlets and asked for their advertising rates. This allowed him to ascertain what his prospects were willing to pay to promote themselves to potential customers. When he talked to these potential sponsors, he had a rationale for the price he was asking, and it was in line with what the business owners were paying elsewhere, although it also factored in the difference in quality between his audience and the audiences for the advertising media the prospects were already using.

The following list suggests some ways to gather information about your competitors.

TIPS

- Go to a newsstand. Find the magazines that your audience would probably enjoy. Write down the titles, and go on-line to uncover information about their readership. How big is their subscriber base? How frequently do they reach their subscribers and other readers. Can you uncover their advertising rates?

- Go to local events. Which sponsors from your community are there? What kind of presence do they have? They will be your prospects too.

- Participate in raffles, sweepstakes, redeeming local coupons, and giveaways. Pay attention to what happens as you participate so you understand what kind of follow-through is being delivered to advertisers and sponsors.

- Go to a local business that is a sponsor with a bounce-back coupon (a redeemable offer that "bounces" the customer back to the retailer or manufacturer to make a discounted purchase). Watch the reaction. Pick a slow time to savor what you'll see. Is the person at the counter pleased, surprised, or indifferent to the coupon? The answer will tell you what value the business places on it. Bounce-back coupons have a higher value than sponsor logos because they drive customers to the sponsoring company, and the sponsor gets the immediate gratification of knowing its investment worked.

Competitors exist in all situations. That's a positive sign; it tells you there is enough demand to support multiple offerings. Too often we view competitors as a threat, but when nonprofits are seeking sponsorship they should understand that competition is useful. If an auto dealership is sponsoring a regional jazz festival, for example, it will likely be open to sponsoring the symphony as well. That is why it is important to foster a healthy sense of competition among the like-minded sponsorship seekers in your area. Share information and ideas. "You don't have to open your kimono, but sharing what works is a good idea. It makes the whole sector more attractive," explains Candace Renwall (2002), executive director of the Chicago Software Association. Renwall has hosted my firm's Sponsorship Bootcamp for a network of other technology associations. Part of her objective is to make technology associations popular among sponsors. To reach this objective, she needs to have a number of technology associations offering sophisticated programs to sponsors.

TIP

Your public librarian can be of enormous help in researching the competition. The information age has made them master navigators. They often have media guides, local business information, and contact names, as well as access to multiple databases that can save you precious time. The International Events Group publishes the *IEG Sponsorship Report,* a newsletter that occasionally posts the prices sponsors have paid for their affiliations with specific properties. Subscriptions are pricey but worth the investment. But, first, ask if your local library subscribes.

Use the form in Worksheet 3.1 to organize your research as you track the competitors in your region.

Putting a Value on Your Intangible Assets

As described in Chapter One, your organization can deliver intangible assets that are of great value to a sponsor because they involve human feelings and reactions that the sponsor wishes to engage on its own behalf. The presence of these intangible assets separates sponsorship from other types of marketing or advertising. Moreover, they can affect sponsors' emotional response to your property. The value of these assets is harder to measure than the value of the tangible assets and prone to subjectivity. After a decade of analyzing sponsorship programs, I have identified the essential intangibles—the ones that increase the market value of a sponsorship deal—and developed a formula that suggests how much more a deal is worth when various levels of intangibles are added to the tangible benefits.

Worksheet 3.2 will help you assess the degree to which your sponsorable property offers each of these essential intangibles and calculate and interpret your score. Exhibit 3.2 contains an example of the scoring process.

WORKSHEET 3.1

Analysis of Competitors

List the competitors (events, programs, and other sponsored arrangements) you wish to research in the first column of the table. For each one, identify the fee the sponsor paid ("sale price"), the sponsor, the estimated number of people the sponsor reached through this sponsorship deal, and any other benefits the sponsor appears to have received. After completing your research calculate the average sale price received by this group of competitors.

Competitors	Sale Price	Sponsor	Audience Reach (Estimated)	Apparent Benefits to Sponsor (Signage, Exclusivity, Product Display, and So On)

Average sale price $ _____ .

Assessing Intangibles

A. Scoring

The first part of this worksheet describes eight intangible assets in terms of their importance to sponsors. After reading each description, rank the degree to which your sponsorable property delivers this asset, on a scale of 1 to 10, with 1 being the lowest score (compared to other properties, yours delivers very little) and 10 being the highest score (compared to other properties, yours delivers a great deal). In addition to completing a separate worksheet for each of your properties, you may wish to complete a separate worksheet for each sponsor if your prospective sponsors vary in attitudes and needs.

1. **Name recognition.** Sponsors benefit when the nonprofit property they sponsor is well known and well regarded in the sponsor's community or any other community the sponsor wishes to reach.

   Score for name recognition (1–10) _____

2. **Exclusivity.** A sponsor will often pay a premium when the nonprofit property it sponsors can ensure that it will be the only company of its type involved with the property.

   Score for exclusivity (1–10) _____

3. **Audience appeal.** Accuracy is everything in marketing. The sponsor is under pressure to hit a precise target when marketing. It is essential that the audience you deliver contains the people the sponsor wants to reach and that your sponsorable property is one of the best ways to reach that audience. For instance, polo, dressage competitions, and cultural events deliver high net worth individuals to sponsors better than other types of marketing do. These buyers are notoriously hard to reach, selective with their time, and passionate about their lifestyle pursuits. The nonprofit with this audience delivers a great deal of audience appeal to the sponsor who needs to reach these people.

   Score for audience appeal (1–10) _____

4. **Simplicity of involvement.** For this book I interviewed eighteen decision makers at companies that engage in sponsorships. This was during a time of deep personnel cuts at most major companies. Overworked and in fear of being downsized, these decision makers spoke of the pressure to deliver results with little or no staff. "Make [the sponsorship event] turnkey. I cannot get involved with sending anyone from my team. Deliver for me or I can't sponsor you," declared one decision maker who was splitting her time between community affairs and marketing.

   Score for simplicity of involvement (1–10) _____

5. **Track record.** Nothing succeeds like success. Sponsors rarely take chances on other organizations' untried material. Instead, they invest in organizations and properties where other sponsors are already engaged and seem to be happy and well served.

   Score for track record (1–10) _____

WORKSHEET 3.2, Cont'd

6. **Media draw.** A property's ability to attract unpaid media and to deliver a share of the advertising it does for its event or offering has several benefits for a sponsor. Media coverage delivers the sponsor's connection to the property to a wider audience than the audience that attends or directly participates in the offering. Media coverage increases the number of guaranteed impressions the sponsor's name or logo achieves. Editorial coverage that links your property with a sponsor can have a profound impact on the sponsor's brand identity in the public mind.

Score for media draw (1–10) _____

7. **Identity and imagery.** Some organizations grow to become cultural icons, symbols of something much larger than their daily work. For example, the Olympics, the Red Cross, and Reading Is Fundamental all have a multilayered symbolism and bring many positive human qualities and abilities to people's minds. In addition, some organizations present or support work that symbolically reflects a specific intangible aspect of the sponsor's product or service: for example, dance suggests precision performance; the visual arts suggest creativity, style, innovative thinking; music suggests luxury, precision timing; running suggests independence, a go-getter spirit; sailing suggests intensive teamwork.

Score for identity and imagery (1–10) _____

8. **Solid management.** Sponsor decision makers may find it difficult to engage in business deals with individuals who look and behave very differently from their own colleagues. Sponsors place a premium on a management team that speaks their language, tracks and reports outcomes, and provides expertise to fill in gaps in their own thinking. Over time, a long-standing sponsorship arrangement begins to look like a marketing partnership in which each side takes an avid interest in the other's success on many levels.

Score for solid management (1–10) _____

B. Calculating and Interpreting Your Score

1. Enter the scores for the eight items in the table that follows and total the scores.

Asset	Score
Name recognition	
Exclusivity	
Audience appeal	
Simplicity of involvement	
Track record	
Media draw	
Identity and imagery	
Solid management	
TOTAL	

WORKSHEET 3.2, Cont'd

2. Locate your score in the left-hand column of the following table. The number in the right-hand column gives you your *multiplier,* the percentage by which your sponsorable property's intangible assets are likely to increase its base value (the value of its tangible assets) to the sponsor.

Score	Percentage Increase in Base Value
80–70 points	50%
69–50 points	40%
49–30 points	30%

3. Calculate increase in base value.

   $ _____ $ (base value) + (_____ [multiplier] × $ _____ [base value]) =
   $ _____ $ (total value to sponsor).

EXHIBIT 3.2

Assessment Scoring Example

Asset	Score
Name recognition	7
Exclusivity	5
Audience appeal	3
Simplicity of involvement	7
Track record	1
Media draw	9
Identity and imagery	8
Solid management	10
TOTAL	50

Score	Percentage Increase in Base Value
80–70 points	50%
69–50 points	40%
49–30 points	30%

The percentage increase in base value for the hypothetical sponsorable property in this example is 40%. Therefore, if the property's base value were $15,000, its likely value with the intangibles factored in would be $21,000:

$$ \$15,000 + (.40 \times \$15,000) = \$21,000 $$

In this case, because sponsors commonly deal in round numbers, a sponsee would round the number down to $20,000.

Identifying Additional Pricing Factors

The factors listed in Exhibit 3.3 are also beneficial to your property's bottom-line value. Although they are not must-haves, the presence of any one of these factors can make your organization more attractive to a sponsor.

EXHIBIT 3.3

Additional Pricing Factors

Item	Benefit to Sponsor
• Introduction to desirable cosponsors	• Opens doors for sponsors to other executives.
• Substantial market size	• Gives the sponsor access to more of the desired audience.
• Participation of a retail sponsor	• Expands promotional opportunities for other sponsors.

In addition, a fit with the personal values of sponsor decision makers can make a difference. This factor is a wild card. Sponsors will deny that it matters, as will industry experts who comment on sponsorship but don't actually have to sell and manage deals. Why? Because it seems undisciplined and self-serving to be investing marketing dollars to validate a personal value or preference of the CEO or other members of senior management. Yet it happens every day. A marketing director for one of the top five accounting firms once lamented to me: "Every year I put in the check request for our golf sponsorship and I know it drives no new business for us. I know I could be more strategic, but the partners love it. No one is going to walk down the hall and tell me to kill the stupid golf deal. They are going to reach for their putters and tell me what a great job I'm doing!" This is not business logic at work here, but it is part of the alchemy of decision making. If this factor is not in your favor, you cannot force it to change, and it is hard to anticipate decision makers' personal preferences prior to the sales process. But do be aware that this factor exists.

Establishing Implementation Costs

Servicing and fulfillment expenses are real costs. Sponsors understand that. If they make special requests, they expect to be charged the related hard costs—postage and handling, for example, or equipment or tent setup. In the case of a labor-intensive event where your volunteers are working on behalf of the sponsor to distribute product information or samples, it is appropriate to calculate the total value of that labor based on the minimum wage (and then calculate the charge to the sponsor as described in the accompanying tip).

TIP

The industry standard for the implementation cost that can be absorbed by a sponsor is to calculate it at 10 to 15 percent of the total cost of implementation. Factor this cost in, and show it to sponsors, so they know it will not be charged to them elsewhere.

Valuing Media

Most sponsorship packages include paid media promotions. The nonprofit organization or sponsorable property invests cash to buy media time or space, or media donate time or space to the nonprofit for use in promoting its event or cause. Either way, these media promotions are tangible and guaranteed, as opposed to media exposure achieved through public relations, which is considered "unmeasured" media. The guaranteed media in your package are significant to a sponsor. Yet you cannot simply pass the full cost through to the sponsor because the sponsor is receiving exposure only in a portion of the promotion. In print advertising, for example, the sponsor's name commonly appears at or near the top of the nonprofit's ad, although it may also sometimes appear near the bottom. The size and positioning of the sponsor's name and logo affect the value of the advertising to the sponsor and hence what you can charge for it. The industry standard is 10 percent of the total book rate for the ad. For example, if you have paid $16,000 for print advertising in which the sponsor's name and logo appear, the value to the sponsor is $1,600.

Another tool in calculating the cost of media is to consider *cost per thousand* (CPM). This is a basic measure of marketing and media efficiency. It is the fundamental measure, understood industry-wide, for comparing competing media. It represents the cost of exposing an advertising message to 1,000 viewers or readers or other target audience members. It is calculated as follows:

$$CPM = total\ cost \div total\ audience\ (in\ thousands)$$

A Tool to Calculate Your Property's Value

Worksheet 3.3 contains a simplified formula for calculating the value of assets you are offering a sponsor. Exhibit 3.4 presents an example of the formula worked out for a hypothetical nonprofit. Consult your completed versions of Worksheets 2.1 and 2.2 for items you may wish to add to Worksheet 3.3.

WORKSHEET 3.3

Value Estimation Formula

To estimate the value of the assets your property offers a sponsor, complete the calculations on the following form for as many items as apply to your property. Use the blank lines to add assets that your property offers but that are not shown here.

Item	Calculation	Sponsor Price
Cost of your media buy (@ 10% of total purchased media)		
Database (cost per membership list name)		
Event impressions (posters, brochures, T-shirts, and so on) (CPM)		
Hard costs (tent rental, catering, and so on)		
Fulfillment labor (@ 10% of total event or project cost)		
SUBTOTAL (base price)		
Intangibles percentage		
TOTAL		
Average comparable price		
RECOMMENDED PRICE		

EXHIBIT 3.4

Value Estimation Example

Item	Calculation	Sponsor Price
Cost of your media buy (@ 10% of total purchased media)	$75,000 × .10	$7,500
Database (cost per membership list name)	25,000 names @ .17 each	$4,250
Event impressions (posters, brochures, T-shirts, and so on) (CPM)	(1,000,000 ÷ 1,000) × 5.00 per 1,000	$5,000
Hard costs (tent rental, catering, event management, and so on)		$25,500
Fulfillment labor (@ 10% of total cost to produce the event or project)	$25,500 × .10	$2,550
SUBTOTAL (base price)		$44,800
Intangibles percentage	$44,800 × .40	$17,920
TOTAL		$62,720
Average comparable price:	(Based on no less than 7 comparisons)	$58,000
RECOMMENDED PRICE		$60,000

Conclusion

Once you have completed this exercise, you will know the places where your answers are clear and you are positive you can deliver. These are your areas of strength. Where you struggled, perhaps because your organization doesn't offer a particular asset, you have identified a place to grow. (Or perhaps you'll never provide that type of asset because it's not what your organization is about and you can just take it off the table.) When new assets become available, they can be added into the pricing equation. The point is to emerge with clear and realistically priced areas of strength. They will become the key selling points that you will highlight in your sponsorship proposal, which is the subject of the next chapter.

Part Two

Engaging with Sponsors

THIS SECTION DEALS with the practical aspects of sponsorship seeking, including proposal development, prospecting for sponsors, and pitching your offer to a sponsor. The information and tools in these chapters represent the reality of the work of sponsorship seeking:

- Attracting sponsors to your nonprofit

- Working with your board

- Succeeding at cold calls

- Handling a sponsor meeting—what to do and say

- Negotiating and closing a deal

- Staying on top of legal and tax concerns

- Keeping sponsors happy and coming back for more

Tips, tools, and case studies illuminate the process step-by-step to give you a road map for your journey.

Chapter 4
Drafting the Proposal

A WELL-PREPARED sponsorship proposal achieves what any good sales document does—it facilitates a decision. You will be preparing your proposal so you can use it in one of these three ways with a sponsor:

- To obtain another meeting
- To leave behind following a meeting to facilitate the discussion among several decision makers
- To deliver as follow-up to a meeting where you were requested to address specific issues

Although the content of a proposal might vary based on your situation and the sponsor's needs and interests, there are guidelines that apply to all situations. This chapter will help you turn the information you have gathered about your property into a compelling communications device that propels you into deal making.

Facilitating a Sponsor's Decision Making

For any piece of writing to persuade a person to act, its content must be considered from that person's perspective. The following sections will help you anticipate what the sponsor needs from your proposal.

Help in Visualizing the Offer

Because good sponsorship offers have a human element, it's your job to bring that value to life. It isn't easy for a corporate executive sitting at a desk to imagine the sights and sounds of the experience you are proposing for consideration. Include photos, drawings, diagrams, maps, and charts that help the decision maker visualize your event at a glance. In any sales process you make strides when buyers can picture themselves using the product or service. The same is true when you are selling sponsorship.

Help in Grasping the Offer Quickly

Use crisp, bulleted remarks surrounded by lots of white space to make your arguments. Headlines should be brief but should also suggest a main idea in the form of a complete, qualitative remark—for example, "Superior customer hospitality."

Aim to be clear and compelling. Put your most persuasive sales arguments upfront. That way, the sponsor's decision makers will understand your value even if they don't read to the end, which they rarely do! Here's an example of a brief but powerful argument I developed for the National PTA:

> *We <u>Are</u> the Pulse of America's Parents*
>
> *The national Parents and Teachers Association is the nation's largest, most trusted, and most widely recognized parent organization with over 6.5 million members in 26,000 local units whose volunteers advocate for children and encourage parents to get involved in schools. We invite you to experience the power of the PTA at its height during Back-To-School.*

Help in Seeing the Fit

Is your audience the right audience? Sponsors want a tight match between your audience and their target audience. Demographics and psychographics are impressive to sponsors and help them see the fit. This is how they judge all marketing initiatives. Also, presenting current data on your audience proves that your organization cares about tracking information.

Going beyond statistics, you might also offer profiles of your audience as people. This proves that you have insight the sponsor can tap into. Sponsors throw away proposals every day that are little more than demographic charts and tables. The proposals with stopping power define the nonprofit's audiences in both factual and emotional terms, as this description of PTA moms does:

> *PTA Member Profile*
>
> *Who is the new PTA mom?*
>
> - *Busy contemporary woman with traditional values*
> - *Volunteers for 2 or more activities to "belong"*
> - *Drives a 5 year old mini-van*

- *Votes*
- *Shops with coupons*
- *Budgets the family money*
- *Does research for purchases over $50*

Help in Gaining More Visibility for Sponsor Brand

Sponsors look for public relations and paid media exposure. In fact, now that the sponsorship industry is maturing, properties without a paid media campaign complementing their offering will find it difficult to compete for a sponsor's attention.

Sponsors also look for names and logos that confer a benefit in public relations or increased visibility when linked to the sponsor's name. But be realistic about the value of your organization's name and logo. The more established a property, the larger its scope and reach, and the bigger its identity in the marketplace, the more potential it has to be sponsored. Such properties command significant sponsorship fees, and their names and logos are prized. Properties that are new to the market and events or organizations with limited reach are not so lucky. If your property or event falls into the latter category, avoid loading benefits that don't ring true into the proposal. "It was a joke to get a proposal from a property we had never heard of before, and they were offering the right to use their marks and logo," commented a seasoned marketing director from a financial services company. However, when Rock the Vote was just an idea on a whiteboard, its producer made a case for the value of its marks by discussing its relationship to MTV, which guaranteed significant airtime to make it a high-profile project overnight.

Help in Selling

Ultimately, sponsors want to sell their products. Will they be able to sell on-site or through your channel of members or volunteers? Can they have access to your database or include their brochures in your mailings? Is there a way they can place their new product on-site to stimulate the intent to buy among your participants? If you are serious about getting a sponsor, you must understand and accept that a sponsorship property is a solution to a business problem. This is a commercial rather than a philanthropic endeavor. The number one challenge for any company is successfully answering the question, How can we do more business? So describe your benefits in terms of how they help a sponsor sell more products or services. This is challenging for most nonprofits. It means commercializing the way you talk about the people your organization serves and the impact your organization has on the world.

The Proposal Kit

The proposal kit consists of introductory pieces and a set of interchangeable pieces that make up the proposal itself. Which pieces will lead and which will act as background support depends on the sponsor and the sponsor's business category. Overall, the typical proposal kit contains the following items (described in the general order in which the sponsor is likely to encounter them):

Mailing Envelope

This can be a preprinted envelope with a teaser message. Its main function is to attract attention. If it is attractively designed and made of heavy stock, sponsors may continue using it as a file to store your materials. I have seen sponsors walk into meetings carrying the proposal kit in its envelope with other notes and research shoved into it.

The mailing envelope may be used as the delivery device, but nonprofits also commonly deliver their envelopes via Federal Express because sponsors are more likely to open Federal Express packages. If you are on a budget and can't afford an eye-catching mailing envelope, then by all means spring for the Federal Express envelope to hold all your proposal items.

Offer Letter

The offer letter is a must. More than just a business formality, an offer letter introduces you, your organization's representative, as an individual, thereby engaging the sponsor on a personal level. In a digital age, "Never underestimate the power of good analog," reasons Guy Kawasaki (1999, p. 134), author of *Rules for Revolutionaries.* A thoughtfully written offer letter is good analog.

The offer letter should achieve four things:

- Establish or reinforce rapport
- Introduce the key sales argument
- Summarize sponsor benefits
- Request an action or explain next steps

Exhibit 4.1 presents an offer letter my firm developed for Y-Me National Breast Cancer Organization that worked very well for this nonprofit.

EXHIBIT 4.1

Sample Offer Letter

April 6, 1999

Ms. Jill Weaver
Director of Marketing
ABC Insurance Company
2775 Sanders Road
Suite 707
Northbrook, IL 60062

Dear Jill,

Each year at this time, we reach out to corporate leaders like yourself to join the National Breast Cancer Prevention Organization as an Official National Partner and reach 500,000 Americans who will share your company's commitment to the fight against breast cancer.

Today, 2.6 million women are living with breast cancer. The disease encircles the families and friends of these women, and binds them in their determination to conquer the disease. While there is still no cure for cancer, there is hope for survival. That's what our organization represents.

The National Breast Cancer Prevention Organization is a lifeline for men and women whose lives are touched by breast cancer, offering support, education, and information. Our national network reaches into people's lives and communities with services and peer counseling that form a safety net to help women beat the disease.

By joining forces with us, you join a powerful movement that has captivated American consumers and become a proven player in motivating employees, customers, and retailers.

Our corporate partnership program provides all the relevance of local involvement by our affiliates in five major markets, plus the impact of a national media campaign—including award-winning print and television spots developed for us by Foote, Cone and Belding.

More important, your involvement supports a lifeline for thousands of women who find their way to survival with our help. We invite you to share in the power of that most profound human victory by becoming a National Partner.

Please consider the enclosed sponsorship guide a place for us to begin. Our goal is to collaborate with our partners to develop extraordinary promotional programs that raise mutual awareness and ignite local action.

I will be following up next week to hear your thoughts. In the meantime, I look forward to the opportunity to work with you.

Sincerely,

Mary Doe
Sponsorship Director
National Breast Cancer Prevention Organization

Front Cover

The cover sheet, or title page, should tease the reader's interest with memorable facts or headlines. To get ideas, visit a newsstand and peruse the business magazines to pick up clues about phrases and callouts that make you want to read what's inside. This magazine cover writing style will work for you as well. I developed the following for an American Library Association proposal cover:

- *We have more stores than McDonald's.*
- *We are the nation's largest information infrastructure reaching coast-to-coast.*
- *We enroll more children in reading programs than any sports program.*

  We are America's libraries . . .

Proposal

The proposal itself, as mentioned earlier, is a group of interchangeable items that can be assembled to suit the situation. Each of the following plays a different role in persuading the sponsor to consider the opportunity.

The Body—What's the What

The proposal body is the core of the offering. It should describe the sponsorable property in one solid nugget and then list the key selling points. This nugget is concise. It communicates the positive impact your property has on people's lives. Comparable to an elevator speech, it is the one minute you have to tell the sponsor what your property does and who benefits from it. For example, the annual Bumbershoot Arts Festival in Seattle describes itself this way:

> *Bumbershoot is the Northwest's own artrageous four-day party, where Carnivale meets Concert Hall. The last true celebration of summer, Bumbershoot remains the greatest showcase of eclectic and excellent art. A place where 2,500 artists stalk the stages, grace the galleries and choreograph one of the most fun, wacky parties on the planet.*

A quantitative number for the attendance would make this superb description even better. However, it captures the essence of the event perfectly.

The core of the proposal should also communicate the key selling points. These will vary depending on your property. Selling points are your tangible and intangible assets, those aspects of your property that delivers commercial value to the sponsor, whether it be goodwill, sales opportunities, or heightened visibility. Most proposals list five to ten selling points, with a thumbnail description of ways the sponsor can make use of them. The top three selling points should be listed first.

Here are three common top selling points:

- Breadth of reach: the size of your audience and its geographical scope.

- Means for interacting with the audience: events, direct mail, test-drives, or major media coverage of the event. Place the sponsor at the site: "Your identity will ride with ours as our athletes are interviewed by major networks."

- Prestige of your offering or audience: exclusivity is a big driver in any sale, and prestige is its cousin. The following qualifiers all effectively express an organization's prestige.

> "The premiere organization for reaching parents"—National PTA
>
> "North America's most important film event for independent directors"—Sundance Film Festival
>
> "The world's most revered showcase for modern art"—Museum of Modern Art
>
> "The world's largest block party is also the most popular singles event in the entire metro area"—St. Patrick's Block Party in Chicago
>
> "Heralded by the New York Times as the best jazz festival in America"—San Francisco Jazz Fest

Exhibit 4.2 shows how the key selling points might be expressed for a hypothetical national cause aimed at youth development.

Fact Sheet

Another proposal component is the fact sheet. The fact sheet is the sponsor's touchstone. Sponsors use this tool to quickly size up the property and grasp the practical aspects at a glance. Sometimes it can stand alone. For instance, when you cold-call a sponsor's decision maker, she may ask you to fax something right away so she can determine whether more conversation is warranted. The fact sheet plus the sheet with your organization's demographics (described next) can be enough to clinch a meeting. An example of a fact sheet is shown in Exhibit 4.3.

Demographics and Psychographics

Demographic and psychographic information about your organization's audience is vital. Sponsors will not consider a serious commitment to your property without it. Many nonprofits have learned this and in some cases have taken poetic license with their data, embellishing the facts with hyperbolic

EXHIBIT 4.2

Sample Key Selling Points

What Your Sponsorship Achieves

Generate Leads and Open Doors

Create interest and open doors with special giveaways and a custom sweepstakes program. Our popular tool kits for parents with teens are tools your sales team can use as valuable gifts for their prospects.

Build Your Brands and Foster Loyalty

Your tie with us lends credibility and offers content that allows you to educate your customers in new ways about subjects they care about. Leverage your investment when you carry our messages on or in customer information, statements, your Web site, your advertising.

Position Yourself Against Your Competition

You will be the sole sponsor in your category. By taking advantage of an exclusive opportunity, you differentiate your services and virtually shut out the competition.

Gain Powerful Advertising and Media Exposure

Our media partnership with MYV delivers 30,000,000 households targeted at teens, a $500,000 media value. Company name and logo featured prominently on all press materials and program collaterals drives an estimated 47 million additional impressions.

Direct Market to Targeted Audiences

Utilize our database of 75,000 teen girls and boys to send your information, coupons, and special offers. Here is how it works: we'll include your materials in our mailings or coordinate special mailings to participating organizations, schools, local leaders. (Sponsor covers handling costs.)

Get Customized Research and Measured Outcomes

- Include your questions in our Roper Starch Worldwide survey to gauge effectiveness, awareness, and attitudes toward your company.
- Collaborate with us on research that gathers new insights on boys and girls, the results of which we copromote to the media to drive unpaid media impressions.
- Updates and summary reports help you gauge return-on-investment.

Network with Cosponsors and Opinion Makers

Use your VIP package as a powerful incentive for your sales team. We invite your guests to our celebrity events for memorable meet-and-greets.

EXHIBIT 4.3

Sample Fact Sheet

DePaul University Centennial Celebration At-a-Glance

Who	100-year-old University committed to opening wider educational opportunities to Chicago, the nation, and the world based on the principles of innovation, service to others, and hard work.
What	Centennial Celebration
Where	Various areas of Metropolitan Chicago
When	Festivities kick off September 2002 and run through 2003.
Why	A comprehensive, integrated marketing platform for product introduction, product trial, and customer relations among general audiences and key influentials.
Centennial Highlights	Year-long paid media campaign with sponsor ID
	Centennial Convocation, McCormick Place (President Bill Clinton invited speaker)
	DePaul Festival of the Arts
	Centennial Laureate Speaker Series (Newsworthy international figures will be invited to speak with private receptions to follow.)
	City-wide Public Service Day and Picnic
	Interactive Marketing Symposium
	Charity Golf Marathon
Value-Added	Sponsor visibility in guaranteed print, radio, Web site, and outdoors VIP and Hospitality Packages
	Employee Hospitality Packages
	Preferential vendor agreements, employee and intern recruitment
Investment	Sponsorships range from $25,000–$10,000
How	312-XXX-XXXX 312-XXX-XXXX fax

Source: Reproduced with the permission of DePaul University.

language. Stick to the facts; let your well-researched data speak for themselves. This makes you credible.

Testimonials from Previous Sponsors

There is a "me too" factor in marketing. Sponsors want to join a successful endeavor, and one way they gauge that success is to see whether other known brands are already sponsoring your property. Consider also that access to your cosponsors can be very enticing. If a sponsor's decision maker sees one of the company's prospects on your roster of sponsors, he or she will have added motivation to invest. The testimonials page should be more than a list of companies or logos. It should include endorsement remarks that both answer objections you anticipate from prospects and emphasize the top motivations all sponsors share. For example:

Objection: Will it really help me sell?

"Our tie with this event was a key motivator for our sales associates. We turned 6% more in sales that we directly attribute to our sponsorship."
    —*Brand Manager, ABC Beverage Company*

Objection: Will it be easy to implement?

"This is our third year with the event. We like the support we get from very professional event managers who make our lives easy."
    —*Director of Public Relations, LMN Financial Services*

Objection: Will I gain more visibility?

"The press coverage alone was a boon. Not to mention the way we were touted in all their advertisements and signage."
    —*Director of Marketing, XYZ Computer Company*

Media Clips

Media clips included with your proposal demonstrate your organization's prestige and how well known it is. Proof of media coverage makes you a going concern with proven appeal. Public relations is a tricky business. A company can spend a great deal of money attempting to gain coverage from the press, whether for a new product or some other innovation, and achieve little return. However, the media are more likely to cover events and alliances that deliver noncommercial value to audiences. This coverage is especially valuable for sponsors who hold naming rights or title sponsorship. The Billabong World Surfing Tour, the Sears Theater Fever Festival, and Marshall Field's Sundays in the Park at Ravinia are all event names reflecting title sponsorship. The media must incorporate the sponsor's name in covering the event because it is part of the actual name of the event.

There are a variety of ways to represent your media exposure. The most common approach is to include a few pages of press clips and a list of the radio and television outlets that covered your event or program. Bloomingdale's (Keating, 2002), for example, considers media coverage it receives for its cross-promotions with Hollywood and Broadway to be a key selling point when approaching manufacturers to buy in to these promotions. It presents booklets containing color copies of the print media the promotions have generated. These are never just sent to sponsors; instead they are given to sponsors during meetings, for them to peruse on the spot.

Summary of Rights and Benefits

The benefits summary is a punch list of the rights and rewards of being a sponsor. Seasoned sponsorship seekers put this summary closer to the back than the front of the proposal kit. "I got benefits burn-out after awhile," said Laurie McCullough (2002), a former communications manager at MCI, referring to the endless litany of rights and benefits that some sponsees assume will translate into selling points. The purpose of the benefits summary is to let the sponsor know there is important value to be had in the relationship. If the proposal has done its job, then by the time the sponsor's decision maker has reached the benefits summary, she or he is scanning them for confirmation that this is a great opportunity, not wrestling with the larger value proposition. Exhibit 4.4 shows a sample summary.

EXHIBIT 4.4

Sample Summary of Rights and Benefits

- Full Promotional Rights/Official Designation
- Exclusivity
- Sponsorship of Local Units That Sign Up for the Promotion
- Customizable Retail Extensions
- Advertising Exposure and Media Extensions
- Signage
- Cross-Promotion with Cosponsors
- Heightened Visibility
- Direct Communication
- Targeted Customer Interactions

Response Device or Call-to-Action

Sponsorship is a considered purchase, not an impulse buy. It is unlikely that the sponsor would check "YES! I WANT TO SPONSOR YOU TODAY!" immediately after reading your proposal. But it can be important to include a response device for the sponsor who is genuinely intrigued and wants to invite a discovery meeting. So consider adding to your proposal kit a simple postcard or fax-back form that looks something like the one displayed in Exhibit 4.5.

EXHIBIT 4.5
Sample Response Device

☐ YES! I'd like to learn more about the Highland Games.

    Please call me directly at: _____

    Send me more information via e-mail. Here's my e-mail address:

    _____

☐ I am not interested at this time, but keep me on your mailing list.

☐ Sorry, no.

Conclusion: What a Proposal Can't Do for You

A good proposal facilitates a sale. It doesn't take the place of a face-to-face meeting. You might think of it as a script that you and the sponsor's decision maker will follow as you present the opportunity and he or she interacts and asks questions. A proposal substantiates the opportunity and makes it real. Good ones are read carefully by corporate executives. I have known sponsors' decision makers to carry proposals around in briefcases to read on the road. I have seen dog-eared, tattered proposal kits with Post-Its peeking out from pages. Good proposals are blueprints for making something wonderful happen. If you have been thinking of the preparation of your proposal kit as a disagreeable task, now's the time to change that attitude. See it as an opportunity to tell your story from the heart . . . and the head.

Chapter 5

Gaining Access to Sponsors

YOUR SALES STRATEGY should take a two-pronged approach: *push* and *pull*. This chapter will help you tackle the pull side of selling, where the focus is on drawing prospects toward you by creating awareness and generating warm leads, meaning those with whom you have already had some contact or who have expressed interest. The steps described in this chapter are part of the sales alchemy you will need to concoct to get results, so consider applying as many of the tactics described here as you can muster.

Creating Demand

You will improve the odds for obtaining lucrative sponsorship deals, and reduce the wear-and-tear of cold calling, when you make a conscious effort to attract sponsors to you. The first step in this direction is to make prospective sponsors aware of your organization. Better yet, you want to gain recognition for your nonprofit as an organization already working successfully with sponsors. There are many ways to achieve this, from simple tactics to more elaborate marketing and public relations tactics. Here are a few ideas.

Helping Sponsors Network Through Sponsorship Seminars

Sponsorship seminars were fashionable when sponsors were competitively shopping. They still work but for different reasons. The idea is to invite potential sponsors and their advertising agencies to a breakfast seminar for the business community to preview your upcoming season of events and learn about your audience, reach, and promotional muscle. For a major performing arts facility, for instance, the stated objective might be to present information on entertainment trends and consumer leisure habits. Additionally, this seminar lets you showcase the power of your venue or offering. You might, for example, invite a representative of a current sponsor to give a talk on how his or her company benefits from its sponsorship.

Today sponsors are too busy to window-shop. However, the idea of gathering sponsors has merit based on a different principal—networking.

> The Chicago Children's Hospital hosts an annual fall event for the corporate community at which a panel of speakers presents information about new research or initiatives at the hospital. The CEO of the hospital speaks briefly, and usually a corporate executive shares a personal experience he or she has had with the hospital. The event is usually held at a current sponsor's headquarters, and attracts forty to fifty attendees who network afterward and talk about their involvement, or intended involvement, with the hospital.

Attending a nonprofit's seminar with the objective of networking with other sponsors is still attractive to sponsors. If you want to host a sponsor seminar, make sure that your invitation includes the agenda of speakers or panelists and their affiliations. This will help drive attendance.

Building Awareness Through Public Relations

The power of unpaid media exposure is growing. Depending on the sponsor's business category, it can be a sponsor's greatest motivator for working with a nonprofit. Your ability to demonstrate that your cause or event is mediagenic serves a dual purpose: it shows that your organization can attract the visibility the sponsor wants, and it establishes your organization's legitimacy as a going concern. I recommend hiring a clipping agency during the seasons when your organization is very active. Ask a volunteer or intern to create a *press book,* a collection of all your most impressive media placements. This can travel with you to sponsor meetings as part of your show-and-tell, or you can reproduce and bind a collection of clippings into a flip book and use it as part of the proposal kit.

More important, sponsors' decision makers and managers consume the same media as everyone else. Their awareness of your organization or event is the first requirement for making a sale. So any positive media attention your organization attracts can focus sponsors' attention on it also.

Six Simple Ways to Draw Sponsor Attention with Public Relations

1. Work with an advertising agency to create a pro bono media campaign for your organization.

2. Send holiday cards to sponsors.

3. Host special tours, meet-and-greets, or behind-the-scenes events for sponsors.

4. Invite decision makers from advertising and PR agencies to your events.

5. Job swap with a few companies in your area. Trade CEOs for the day. Contact the local media and tell them about the swap.

6. Enter a team in newsworthy races and competitions such as 10K runs and marathons. Make sure the team members wear your organization's name. Invite current sponsors to run with your team.

Working with Corporate Foundations to Gain Access

For years arts organizations and other causes strove, often unsuccessfully, to gain the attention of corporate marketing departments, only to be directed back to the corporate foundations. Although sports sponsors conduct their sponsorship programs from their marketing departments, arts sponsors more commonly center the sponsorship function in the PR department or community affairs department (Quester and Thompson, 2001).

For most nonsports properties, then, a corporation's foundation and community relations or PR departments will be the points of entry. From there, if a relationship can be built with an officer at the foundation, that officer can work from the inside to champion the sponsorship opportunity to the marketing department and to get funds to promote the tie. In this way corporate foundations can make philanthropic investments that are aligned with profit motives and use marketing dollars to raise visibility for the organizations they fund. Here are some practical ways to get assistance from foundation staff.

TIP

- Ask for coaching. The program officer at the corporate foundation is already friendly to nonprofits. In my experience these individuals are mission driven and want to help. When introducing him or her to your project, mention that you think it's a good fit with the marketing focus at the company but that you would need more background to know if it was a precise fit. Ask the program officer if he or she could provide some insight. Keep this request open ended, and accept what you are told.

- Avoid hidden agendas. You will make more progress if you reveal early that your intent is to build a coalition of support with the foundation and the marketing department.

- Be prepared with Plan B. If the foundation rejects a philanthropic request from your organization, try to find out why it felt a lack of fit. Use that conversation to explore a second approach to marketing.

- Ask for a meeting. Sometimes the foundation officer can orchestrate a meeting of foundation staff, marketing staff, and you. If you have a good track record with the foundation, its staff will be more likely to risk setting up such a meeting. Keep in mind that their reputations are at stake when they ask marketing to attend meetings with nonprofits. "Many nonprofits have trouble understanding time and content limitations. They tend to go on and on, until my colleagues' eyes glaze over," remarked Mary Beth Salerno (2002), vice president of American Express Foundation, when I interviewed her.

- Get postmeeting feedback. The foundation officer can also be a resource to tell you how you are doing and what you need to shore up, either in the offering or proposal. Make sure to get in touch within a week of the meeting in order to get feedback while it's still fresh and to ask for advice on how to move forward.

- Once a sponsorship deal is made, keep separate records, but cross-referenced records, for the funds your organization gets from different corporate areas. Be very clear about how much is considered philanthropy dollars and how much is promotional spending. If possible, designate separate in-house accounts for each revenue stream. If there are tangible advertisements required from your organization that go beyond standard recognition for the company's gift, be sure there is a paper trail for this expense also. Inadequate record keeping could result in a situation in which the entire amount received from the company would become taxable under UBIT laws (as discussed further in Chapter Seven).

Some nonprofits maintain completely separate solicitation programs, one for sponsorship and one for corporate philanthropy. As companies continue to aim their philanthropy at achieving profit motives such hard lines will be difficult to justify. If existing trends continue, it will become more common that nonprofits will accept a grant from a corporate foundation to cover hard costs for a project and then receive additional dollars from the marketing department to raise the project's visibility for mutual benefit. As long as all parties are upfront about which dollars are which and how the money can be applied or restricted, these hybrid deals can work to your advantage.

Getting Appropriate Assistance from Your Board

Many nonprofits benefit from having influential board members. Although success in attracting corporate sponsorship is usually the result of having the audience, reach, imagery, and media package that can effectively support a sponsor's business objectives, there is also something to be said for entrée to the right decision makers. One of the best sponsorship deals a music school I know of ever made, for example, was the result of a board member placing a call to a contact in the company's marketing department and asking that person to expect a call from the music school.

Board members should not be asked to make personal solicitation calls to sponsors, as they might do with donors. They should, however, be invited into the process in other ways. Consider giving board members an annual preview that covers goals, strategies, and prospects for the year's sponsorship effort. Then ask for volunteers to make introduction calls to those prospects where they have contacts, and also ask if there are prospects not already mentioned whom a board member knows and would feel comfortable calling to prepare the way for you.

Working with Agencies Hired by the Sponsor

Picture this. It is 5:00 P.M. and your phone rings. The caller is an account executive from an advertising agency who wants to get your organization involved in her client's promotion. Oh, and can you overnight her a packet of information with all the information about your organization? Yes? Great! Oh, and she has a list of all the information she needs from you. It's coming now via e-mail. Have a look and make any additions you'd like. Tomorrow is her deadline. You, thinking this is your big opportunity, scurry around shoveling brochures, fact sheets, and promotional videos into the overnight mailer, which you send at your expense. You stay late to get it all out on time. The following week you call to follow up as agreed. You get voice mail. You get voice mail again the next day. Three weeks later you still have no updates. Two month later this sponsor prospect falls off your tracking sheet. Its new status? Dead end.

To avoid getting caught up in this scenario when you field a call like this, ask the agency representative to set a time for a conference call or agree on a time for him or her to call back. When you deal with such calls on the spur of the moment, you will be susceptible to the agent's frenzy. Ask politely how long he or she will need so you can make sure you can give the call your full attention. This also puts a value on your time.

During the scheduled call ask about the client's background and objectives. Do not send materials to the agency unless you have this client information. This allows you to assemble a thorough and customized sponsorship package. If the agent balks, don't fret. Often the agency doesn't have the contract to represent the sponsor; it is pitching the company and using your organization and materials as part of the presentation. Agencies that actually have a contract will be willing to take time to provide background and answer your questions. Do not send your sponsorship package to the agency without establishing whether the agency is the agency of record with the sponsor. If the agency does have a contract but does not want to reveal the client's name at this stage, at least determine what the client's business category is, so you can avoid a conflict with any of your current sponsors.

How Long Will It Take to Attract a Sponsor?

As you have learned so far, there are many nuances to each organization's sponsorable property and therefore to each sponsorship program. Your timeline should include the preliminary work of assigning value to your assets, putting sales materials in place, and gaining internal sign-off on your packages as well as the work of the actual sales process. The milestones shown in Exhibit 5.1 are taken from DePaul University's Centennial Campaign. The schedule shown for meeting these milestones is aggressive. It was realistic only because the university was so well known among sponsors. Your schedule may well cover a longer time.

Conclusion

Taken separately, none of the steps discussed here will put a sponsor's check on your desk. And certainly, all the awareness in the world will not culminate in a sale unless you push for it. Making sponsorship deals is a contact sport. By combining the tactics in this chapter with the sales advice in the next chapter, you will begin to get results.

EXHIBIT 5.1

Sample Milestones and Timeline for Sponsorship Effort

April

Preparing to Sell

- Agreement on campaign identity and message points
- Finalization of property offerings, packages, media buy, and assets
- Plot sales strategy
- Identification, approvals, and prequalification of prospects
- Refinement of sales materials for final approval
- Detailed research on prospects
- Finalization of desired media mix, reach, and cash budget

May

Selling—Phase 1

- Placement in DePaul vehicles to stimulate sponsor interest
- Preparation and dissemination of offer letters
- Securing sales appointments

June

Selling—Phase 2

- Preparation of tailored proposals
- Making presentations
- Follow-up and appointment setting
- Preparation and dissemination of offer letters
- Securing sales appointments

July–September

Selling—Phase 3

- Preparation of tailored proposals
- Making presentations
- Contract negotiation
- Closing

Chapter 6

Selling, Negotiating, and Closing the Deal

PROPOSALS IN HAND, your colleagues in agreement, you are ready to start actively selling. This chapter deals with the *push* aspect of your sales strategy. In the previous chapters I have been emphasizing that sponsorship deals are *sold*. Some people in the nonprofit sector have trouble using that word; perhaps it's too commercial. Call the process what you wish—when you begin meeting with sponsors, the accepted parlance for what you are doing is *selling*.

This is often the point where nonprofit executives begin to freeze up. The foundations you call on exist to disperse funds to nonprofits. However, for-profit companies look at sponsorship as a marketing investment. And your marketing contact at the corporation from which you are seeking sponsorship may need plenty of convincing that any sponsorship deal is a good idea. His or her job is to advertise the company's products, not give away money to nonprofits.

So most nonprofits are daunted by the multiple challenges of penetrating the fortress of the company to get to the right person and then following through with the meetings and presentations, deal making and agreements. This chapter seeks to demystify that process of getting meetings and then pitching, negotiating, and closing a sponsorship deal.

Understanding How the Deal Will Flow

Every deal has its own nuances. Those aside, there is a typical pattern of activity to the process; I call it *deal flow*. Exhibit 6.1 shows the phases and steps in this flow and will help you visualize how the deal making is likely to unfold.

EXHIBIT 6.1

Step-by-Step Sponsorship Deal Flow

Phase I

Step 1. Sign off internally on sponsor packages and the rights and benefits that accrue.

Step 2. Identify most likely sponsors or sponsor business categories. Research prospects.

Step 3. Meet with any other internal departments that handle procurement or programming and ensure a single line of communication.

Step 4. Separate out any previous or standing exclusive arrangements in the portfolio of current sponsorship deals.

Phase II

Step 1. Send offer letter to prospects.

Step 2. Follow-up by phone to seek appointments. Begin with referrals and warm leads.

Step 3. Conduct in-depth research to prepare for first meetings.

Step 4. Hold first meeting ("discovery meeting"): thirty to forty minutes long to present the opportunity in broad strokes and to gather insights into the sponsor's business objectives. Schedule second meeting (plan for one hour).

Step 5. Send "thanks for the meeting" letter.

Phase III

Step 1. Develop detailed proposals based on research and information gathered at the first meeting and tailored to the business category.

Step 2. Hold second meeting: a full-blown presentation, the rights and benefits package, and any special overlays tailored for that particular sponsor. Gather feedback.

Step 3. Establish next steps.

Step 4. Proceed with agreed-upon steps. Begin negotiations.

Step 5. Prepare agreement (preferably you do this, not the sponsor).

Step 6. Sign and circulate agreement.

Step 7. Begin fulfillment.

Step 8. Send "thank you and welcome aboard" letter or stage kickoff event.

Getting Your First Meeting

If you have done the marketing and public relations work described in the previous chapter, direct contact comes next. Very large, well-known organizations may have sponsors seeking them out and may not have to be proactive. This is rare, however. Proactive selling is more common among properties who receive handsome sponsorship fees. As popular as NASCAR is as a sponsorable property, it has one of the most aggressive sales approaches in the sponsorship industry. For example, Dermott Eagan (2002), director of marketing at Culligan International, explained that "if there is one constant in my job, it is the salesman from NASCAR. He calls me every week." So expect to pick up the phone to get a meeting with a sponsor. And no doubt your best deals will come from your being proactive. First, work through your list of warm leads derived from the work you did in the previous chapter. Then reach out to your second-level prospects, potential sponsors for whom you have no special contacts and no one to smooth your way. The next section will help you handle that outreach.

Taking the Chill out of Cold Calling

Nobody in business looks forward to making cold calls, and in my experience, nonprofits especially disdain the idea of having to cold-call a sponsor. To help people get over cold-call reluctance, I have developed some tools that make the process less onerous. My firm has a division that sets appointments with sponsors, and I have seen firsthand that taking the time to prepare for cold calling improves the odds of getting through tenfold.

As a first step, take the time to prepare a couple of cold-call scripts. They will enhance the quality of your cold calling, which means you will suffer less rejection. Write out what you plan to say on the phone to the receptionist and to the decision maker. Follow these formats as you prepare your scripts:

Dealing with the Receptionist on a Cold Call

- Introduce yourself. Give your name, company, and the name of the executive you are trying to reach.

- Expect to be screened. Don't try to dodge this screening; it only creates resistance. Explain the purpose of your call and repeat the name of the individual you would like to contact. Ask if this person is still the appropriate contact for your purpose. Duties and people change often in businesses.

- Establish rapport. If you can't get through to the executive at this point, take the time to establish rapport with the receptionist. If you have been referred by someone or have some other specific reason for calling this executive or this company, tell him or her.

- Ask questions. If you haven't already established that the person you are calling is the right person for you to talk to, do so now. Does he or she still make sponsorship decisions? What is his or her schedule like? When does he or she tend to be available to take calls? These questions help you qualify the prospect: is this in fact a likely sponsor?

- Set the next step. Give the receptionist a time when you will call back. Note it, and then call back!

Dealing with the Decision Maker on a Cold Call

- Introduce yourself. Give your name, organization, and the purpose of your call.

- Get permission to continue. Is this a good time? If not, ask what time would be better.

- Present an abbreviated version of your elevator speech. Plan what you will say in twenty seconds or less to get the decision maker excited about your offer.

- Overcome common objections. Anticipate objections from the decision maker. Write out the likely objections and your response to each one.

- Engage with questions. Once you have the executive's attention, gather information that is key to determining whether your program is appropriate for the company. Ask what the company is currently doing to take advantage of sponsorship opportunities, and whether it tends to make its sponsorship plans and purchases at particular times. Find out what it wants nonprofits to understand about the way it makes its sponsorship decisions.

- Listen. Ask a question—then listen! Peacefully. The less you talk, the more the executive will tell you.

- Ask for the appointment. Once you have qualified your prospect and determined that the company is appropriate—make the appointment. Offer a specific time, date, and location for the appointment. Tell the person how much of his or her time you expect to take at that meeting.

- Celebrate. Hang up the phone, and dance around your desk.

- Get back on the phone. Call the next prospect while you're on top. Your excitement will be contagious. Channel it.

Cardinal Rules of Cold Calling

People make cold calling disagreeable when they use the call itself to sell. The reason to cold-call is to learn whether it makes sense to communicate further. In my experience a bright and breezy cold call can be pleasant for both parties if you adhere to the following rules:

- Never push too hard.
- Be sincere.
- Listen.
- Keep your energy up (chocolate, hot tea, lit candles, whatever works).
- Accept rejection gracefully. These people are saving you time.

Handling Frustration

Voice mail and automated messaging have changed the cold-call process significantly. It can get frustrating when you spend a few hours calling and never reach a human being. Expect this process to take time. As I mentioned, my firm sets appointments for properties wanting to qualify sponsor leads, so I know firsthand what it takes to cold-call. Here is what to expect in terms of effort and rejection to go from reaching a sponsor's decision maker to closing your deal.

Reaching a sponsor live at her desk	30 phone calls
Gaining a first meeting	10 rejections per 1 success
Gaining a second meeting	3 rejections per 1 success
Gaining a commitment	1 rejection for every success

Conducting Effective Sponsor Meetings

Good selling is all about getting information and using it to solve the buyer's problem. At your first meeting with the prospective sponsor's decision maker, your mission is to discover the fit between your property and the sponsor's needs. Plan to spend a few minutes building rapport with some general conversation. To begin the move into the heart of the meeting, gauge the time available by saying, "I want to respect your time; how much of it do I have for this meeting?" With that, overview the agenda and preview the outcome: "And I'm hoping that by the end of our meeting we will know if we have a fit or not. If we do, then perhaps we will be able to agree on some next steps." This suggestion that you are sensitive to the need for right fit, allows the executive to relax.

Review your sponsorship program. Begin by asking the executive for permission to talk about your organization: "Would it help if I told you a bit more about us?" Then review the offering and the key selling points and demographics. Share a brief sponsor case study if you have one. Then ask about the sponsor's corporate objectives. Incorporate your research: "I know your company produces widgets for automobiles, but I'd like to hear more about the company from you." Guide the executive toward reviewing the company's primary business objectives—what it does or sells and how it goes about this business. Listen. What you learn will be incorporated into the proposal you will customize for this sponsor. Brainstorm a bit with the sponsor's decision maker. "It sounds like you could make use of something that does X. What about a program like our Y event? Let me paint a picture and see if this is close. . . ." By helping the executive visualize a relationship you begin to engage him or her.

Focusing on the Right Fit

Many people assume that having the sponsor's decision maker captive in a face-to-face meeting is the goal. They then huff and puff through the litany of sponsor benefits. But the main effect of this is to wear the executive down. I know; I've tried this and can save you the painful outcome.

Finding mutual benefit is the goal. The more research you do in advance of the meeting, the more likely it is that you'll find the right fit because you will eliminate inappropriate companies. Your research will also help you better manage the meetings you do get because you will ask more insightful questions and you'll be talking about the subject in which the executive is most interested.

Handling Objections

In the first meeting you need to gain the information that tells you whether there is enough fit to pursue more elaborate discussions. Stick to that goal. If you close the meeting after hearing the executive say no but before you have learned why he or she said no, you have not met the goal. First, acknowledge that you heard the no loud and clear. Then reply with something like this: "I respect your clarity. Many companies feel this way today. But since we are here, would you mind giving me a little background so that I can understand your thinking. Under what circumstances could you consider sponsoring our property?" Listen to the objections. Also, ask the executive to describe the sponsor's dream relationship. From there, either you will have a place to begin again or you will realize how far off a good fit you are with what you have to offer.

If there is something the executive misunderstood, you can gently point it out, or if you have something that is being developed that may be a better fit, you can mention it. Whatever you do, do not get defensive. Thank the decision maker and ask him or her if it would make sense for you to check back in six months. Or ask if there is another department of the company that it would make sense to contact.

TIP

Plan to leave something from your organization with the sponsor's decision maker after that first meeting. It might be a T-shirt, water bottle, or mug or a half-price ticket to your venue. It will reinforce your organization's identity. Use your current events and programs to intrigue sponsors; find ways to let them watch how your sponsorship arrangements work by seeing other sponsors in action. This is a great way to keep your organization in the sponsor's mind.

Setting Up the Second Meeting

If you and the decision maker agree that it makes sense to explore a relationship, you will need to establish three things before you walk out the door:

1. Establish who else needs to be present at this second, exploratory meeting.

2. Set a date for the meeting.

3. Discuss the meeting format. Will you walk them through a printed deck of highlights or use a laptop to do a Power Point presentation? Orient the executive so he or she can visualize the meeting.

These steps lock in the second meeting. Sponsors tend to keep appointments when the concrete details are set in advance because they know whom to recruit to the meetings and what to tell them to expect.

Managing the Second Meeting

If you have earned a second meeting, you have established true interest. Congratulations—you have crossed an important threshold. At the second meeting you will present the proposal, which is the basic draft you prepared earlier with tailored bullet points that reflect the input from the first meeting. You will find that every meeting will be different, depending on who is present and what they need to know to make a decision. I used to cause myself great anxiety trying to manage the flow of the meeting in which I presented a proposal. I became more successful when I remained open and flexible. Close the meeting by getting the participants to agree on the next steps.

As you proceed through these early meetings, you will also want to begin cultivating certain habits that will stand you in good stead in all your future work with both prospective and actual sponsors and will help you continue your transformation from charitable fundraiser to sponsorship marketer. I have mentioned most of these abilities in passing in the previous sections, but it's important to focus on them until they become routine to you in your work.

Listen more than you speak. In every interaction with sponsors, use a light touch when it comes to information about the property you are representing. Most sponsors are both busy and bright. A few key points distilled into bullets locks them into your message. "When we want a not-for-profit to make a presentation to management, we have to coach them to keep it brief," explains Mary Beth Salerno (2002) of the American Express Foundation. "We find that they want to lecture our team, which isn't necessary." Two days before any presentation, eliminate half of the points you want to make. The next day, cut them by half again.

Look professional. You never get a second chance to make a first impression. Sponsors want to collaborate with people they can relate to, and your appearance will convey whether or not you have made the effort to fit in.

Ask penetrating questions. It is your job to find the fit between what your organization does and the sponsor's marketing objectives. Ask about the sponsor's business, how the company sells, distributes, and promotes its products. Your line of questioning should move from the concrete to the abstract. Ask simple questions first. "How many employees do you have?" "How many markets are you in?"

Let your curiosity show. Once on a sponsor call to a school supply company I met with the CEO. I asked about the company's packing and shipping operation. I told him I didn't quite understand how it worked. He led me on a tour of the shipping floor. Beaming with pride, he pointed out the environmentally friendly packaging materials he had developed with a local university-based laboratory. I not only established rapport, but gained insight into his values. Later in our negotiations, he would refer to me as, "This is the woman I was telling you about, who wanted to see the shipping room!" It was clear I had made an indelible impression.

Incorporate what you learn in follow-up letters and proposals. This reinforces your sincerity. It also improves the likelihood that the sponsor will see you as a business colleague, not a fundraiser from a charity.

Be responsive. Return calls. Meet deadlines. Not only does this tell the sponsor you are reliable, it generates momentum for your deal flow. This all sounds obvious, but one of the most frequent complaints I hear from sponsors about nonprofit properties is their lack of follow through.

Use time well. When you chair any meeting, begin on time. Always have a written agenda. End promptly, promising to follow up on any unfinished business with people individually or tabling the issue for the next meeting.

Working Through the Negotiation Process

The negotiation process can be exhilarating or painful, and sometimes a bit of both. Overall, how you fare depends on the sponsor's interest in a long-term relationship and how you react during negotiations. Sponsors who take the long view tend to be more collaborative. Those with a more immediate need to fill, especially when your offer is just one of a number of media purchases they are negotiating, may be more likely to take a commodity approach, where the goal is simply to shave costs.

A barrier to smooth negotiations arises when sponsors withhold certain objectives from you or slip them near the end of the process, perhaps when a Johnny-come-lately member of the sponsor's team makes a demand. In either case, the promotional burden on you will broaden as the negotiations move forward because the sponsor will expect to wring more and more opportunity out of the deal.

To keep your deal moving through the negotiation process, keep the following in mind:

Keep your cool. Remember, this is business, not personal. Nonprofit executives are passionate about the causes they represent; don't let this passion mislead you. One possible error, for example, is taking an issue that arises from simple misperception as a moral affront.

> I once had a sponsor's representative ask if the nonprofit's volunteer corps would hand out samples in grocery stores and insert shelf-talkers about the product. He was rather new to sponsorship, so it was my responsibility to gently point out why that wasn't a fit with this group of volunteers. When he demanded it, things got tense. I defused the situation when I moved the conversation away from the tactic and back to the objective he was trying to achieve. We could then collaborate on achieving what he wanted in a different way.

Know your rock bottom price, and stick to it. There is a point at which you will have invested so much time and energy that you will just want the deal to be done. If the negotiation process has eaten away at the value of the deal, and the relationship is dangerously imbalanced, step back for a bit. Take a hiatus of a few days and then review the deal, looking at the numbers and what the partnership achieves for your organization. If it is still not adding up, start making a wish list of things the sponsor can provide in addition to cash that will bring the exchange between sponsor and nonprofit into balance. This wish list flows from your organization's goals and objectives. For instance, can the company give you some of its prepurchased media? Does it have a big golf tournament it can involve your executive director in to introduce him or her to other corporate leaders?

Know your nonnegotiables. If your organization has set up its internal process and sponsorship policies properly, you will have a clear sense of its parameters.

> Once I had a sponsor's advertising agency decide it wanted to create the curriculum collaterals for an after-school literacy program that was a staple for the nonprofit organization involved. Because the nonprofit had done its groundwork beforehand, it had a policy in place that it would maintain control of materials and programs that were central to its mission. So the nonprofit rejected the idea. The agency persisted. I had to go directly to the sponsor's decision maker and tell her that because giving in to the agency would force the nonprofit to override its written policy, the nonprofit was preparing to walk away from the deal. It eventually did so.

Beware of sponsors who withhold information. Some sponsors may not be immediately forthcoming about objectives they think may not be palatable to you. You can waste a lot of time preparing materials and attending meetings only to find out that the deal they want is inappropriate for your organization.

> In the 1990s, a major telecommunications company was looking to partner with one of my clients, a national school-based organization. The company had planned a promotion focused on selling phone cards. It was an outstanding opportunity. There was a major ad buy and a world-class athlete as spokesperson. The only missing ingredient was a cause-related overlay. That's where the nonprofit came in. Given the scope of the promotion, the deal was apt to generate significant revenue for the cause. It was almost too good to be true.

Our first conference calls left me unclear about the tactics and how the cards would be sold. I called my contact back and probed deeper. The sponsor waffled, saying that several tactics were being considered: direct mail, Web transactions, and bill stuffers. The company was still working it all out.

When the description of the deliverables to be included in the agreement finally arrived, there was a clause about the "volunteers and schoolchildren" going door-to-door to sell the cards. Even more surprising was the sentence detailing how the basketball star would be taking a percentage of each card sold. This was a man who could finance an entire school system. Naturally, negotiations were shut down. The nonprofit had no substitute to offer for what the sponsor saw as the core of the agreement: free labor from volunteer moms and kids. Weeks had been wasted.

So beware of the sponsor who treats you like an innocent from a charitable organization. Some sponsors, or more commonly their advertising agencies, give nonprofits little credit for having any business acumen. If sponsors suspect that the nature of their proposition will seem too commercial to you or that you simply won't get it, they may try to withhold their true business objectives or sugar-coat them. Stay focused, ask straightforward questions, and seek answers you can understand.

Also, trust your gut. I felt odd about that deal right from the start but kept suppressing it. I wasn't the only one fooled, however. I stand vindicated, I suppose, by the fact that this telecommunications company made U.S. business history when its CEO was indicted for misrepresenting profits and borrowing millions of dollars from the company illegally.

The negotiation process can be kicked off with the presentation of a contract or can occur prior to contract development, which is preferable. Involving an attorney from the beginning can be costly. Try to agree on key points and outline them in writing prior to generating a formal contract for your lawyer to review.

Key Negotiating Points to Consider

- Don't allow sponsors to cap the amount they raise in your name through a cause-marketing tie. If the promotion has a time limit, your organization should benefit for the entire duration of the stated promotional window.

- Retain the right to use sponsor income as you see fit. As long as the package of rights and benefits is fulfilled, sponsors should have no input into how the nonprofit spends the sponsorship fees.

- Specify upfront how in-kind payments will be valued. Unless the in-kind item is truly budget relieving, avoid a dollar-for-dollar valuation. It dilutes the economics of your program and trains sponsors to give you product instead of cash.

- Define sponsor categories narrowly enough to keep revenue potential open. For instance, instead of having one financial services sponsor, split the financial services category into segments so you are free to seek a credit card sponsor, an investment advisor sponsor, a brokerage sponsor, and an insurance company sponsor.

- Control your mailing list. Never release your organization's database in digitized form unless it is to a secured third-party mailing house that makes a contractual commitment to return your data and protect your list.

- Define any costs that the sponsor must bear, such as postage or shipping of samples, and any capital expenditures it will be responsible for, such as permanent signage.

- Limit your organization's fulfillment liability for activities that are the sponsor's responsibility. The contract should state clearly what the sponsor's obligations are in the area of sponsor promotion and it should also state that your organization is not responsible for any lack of performance on the part of the sponsor. For example, the sponsor might be responsible for

    Supplying the official logo artwork on time and within specs

    Delivering samples to your event

    Sending inserts to you to insert in a mailing

    Setting up tables or audiovisual equipment for the sponsor's designated booth

    Staffing the sponsor's booth

Accepting In-Kind in Lieu of Cash

In good economic times it is much easier to land cash deals. In tighter times sponsors will get creative to make a deal happen. Sorting through the variety of in-kind goods and services sponsors offer can be dizzying. To gauge the best values, look first to your own costs. Ideally, a sponsor's in-kind contribution will answer a line item in your organization's budget, either reducing the amount of cash you have to spend overall or freeing up cash you can then spend elsewhere.

Working with Swap Outs

Not everything in your offer package will interest a sponsor. More important, every sponsor likes to feel that you have tailored the program for its individual needs. Be prepared to *swap out* (that is, substitute) assets of similar value. In some cases the sponsor's decision maker will ask you to substitute an asset that has a far greater value than the one it replaces. Be careful.

When you allow sponsors to cherry-pick key assets from a top tier package that sells for more money than the package the sponsor has chosen, you can inadvertently cannibalize the pricing system you have set up. Even if you haven't yet sold that top tier, explain to the executive that "this asset has a much greater value, and it is available exclusively at our top tier. In fairness to the sponsor who will be paying the fee for that tier, I can't offer it to another sponsor, unfortunately. Do you want to look at the top tier again?" If the executive is not interested in the top tier package as a whole, ask if you can get back to him or her with some other ideas. Make sure that you understand the marketing goals the executive thinks the sponsoring company can achieve with that asset, then fall back and think through the options, especially if you are feeling pressured and uncertain. This will keep you from making impulsive swap outs you'll later regret.

Making Media Barter Deals

Instead of seeking cash, it is sometimes advisable to swap an asset for any prepurchased media the sponsor might have. Sponsors can buy their media exposure more efficiently than the typical nonprofit, so they pay less for it and purchase much of it in advance. If your goal is to create more awareness for your organization's event, then accepting sponsor media in place of cash could fulfill a need and might also attract additional, cash-paying sponsors if you can incorporate their identities into these media.

Logically speaking, prepurchased media should be valued at what the sponsor paid for them, not the book rate, but some sponsors will balk at that, and you'll have to decide whether to be rigid or flexible on this issue.

Closing with Commitment

Concluding a string of meetings does not close a deal. Terry Sjodin (2001, p. 122), expert sales coach, defines the close as "the action you want your prospect to take as a result of your discussion." Closing involves two phases: working out the offer and answering all needs and objections. The sales process culminates by asking for the prospect's commitment. Depending on the prospect and his or her decision-making power, the commitment you ask for will vary. Here are some suggestions that may help.

Five Things to Say to Close a Sale

1. "Let me describe how we work with sponsors to get them more visibility. This will give you an idea of what commitments you'll need to make and when. [Describe the process, major media milestones, and major event highlights, or whatever is appropriate.] Does this sound like something you are ready to act on?"

2. "Do you feel you have enough information to make a decision on this?"

3. "Pretty soon we will need to understand whether or not this is shaping up the way it needs to for you to be able to make a commitment. Do you feel we are close to what you need here?"

4. "Most sponsors like to get rolling to gain the most visibility for their investment. We are ready to get to work if you feel ready to commit. What do you think?"

5. "We've enjoyed working with you over these past few meetings. We feel very comfortable with what we've developed with you and ready to commit with an agreement. How about you?"

Don't Celebrate Until You Have the Signed Contract and Deposit

Strange delays can creep into these final phases, even when all the questions have been answered, the concerns have been addressed, and people on both sides have signed off. The sponsor should be ready to sign the contract and cut a deposit check. Yet getting to this point can be harder than you would think. Nobody likes to spend money. Psychologically, the sponsor's decision makers have done the hard work of deciding your property is a good fit, but they still sometimes drag their feet at this point in the game.

There are creative ways to remedy these delays. For instance, build in a ceremony or other event that marks the end point of the close. Invite the sponsor to your headquarters, or you can go to the sponsor's. Make the signing and handing off of the check part of the event. In return, give some of your organization's logoed apparel and mementos to the sponsor's team. Take photographs. Give the sponsor the opportunity to comment (clear this with the sponsor in advance of course). Invite your organization's board members and key staff to the event. Provide refreshments or have the sponsor's core team and yours go to lunch together after the signing.

Growing Pains

As your organization becomes more successful in seeking and signing sponsors, that process may become its own internal industry in the organization. As this case study reveals, no matter how big the sponsorship effort becomes, it's important to ensure that it remains firmly linked to the organization's values and goals.

> I once consulted to a highly influential nonprofit in the early stages of its sponsorship program. This cause was so pure, so beloved, it was akin to a national treasure. Having done the work of assessing its value and creating policies that were approved by all the various governing bodies, it began presenting to sponsors. The results were phenomenal.
>
> Once the effort was up and running, with several sponsors on board, it was clear the nonprofit needed a full-time person in house to manage it. The person hired had extensive corporate credentials in marketing and promotions. He was enthusiastic and eager to prove himself. However, after a few months he confessed to feeling out of sync with the culture. Still, he enjoyed meeting with sponsors and their agencies and in no time built high-profile affiliations and made some friends along the way.
>
> All went well until a sponsor asked that the cause officially endorse the sponsor's product. It was an unusual request, and the language in the policies wasn't completely clear on the matter. This was a judgment call. He agreed to it, and when putting the agreement in front of the organization's president for signature, he made no mention of it.
>
> The sponsor-paid television and print spots began rolling and visibility was sky-high. Everyone was elated. Then came the equal and opposite reaction. A week later the *New York Times* had a front-page story about the grand old organization that had sold out. Television coverage followed print. It grew ugly before it blew over. The upshot was that the organization's good name, the very asset that was most valuable, was severely tarnished.

The first lesson to be learned here is that another person in your organization, someone other than the chief negotiator, should always review the final deal. This person might be a level-headed volunteer who is a lawyer, an in-house legal counsel, or a business manager. The point is to get a reality check from someone else who knows your organization. Ideally, you want to use your attorney for each deal, but that gets very expensive. There are ways to avoid heavy legal costs, however, such as having a lawyer tweak an agreement template each time. If the contract is from the sponsor and has new language that is hard to fathom, then by all means use your attorney. Better to be safe.

Also, avoid being blinded by corporate mystique when hiring a sponsorship director. Probe for his or her philosophies and appreciation for what you do and how you do it. Many nonprofits are impressed with corporate credentials. In some cases that response is deserved, but also keep in mind that some people leave corporate jobs yearning to do "something more meaningful" yet never succeed in fully integrating themselves into the values, culture, and nuances of the nonprofit environment. They then can become disillusioned and frustrated.

Conclusion

Once the building blocks are in place to grow your sponsorship program, your organization will automatically be more visible and more successful at attracting people to the cause. Your work will become easier. Prospects will take your calls, and doors will start opening. You will generate momentum.

As you work at this process, remember to enjoy yourself. The job of finding sponsors is loaded with rejection. Over time your self-esteem can take a beating. You cannot attract resources when you are tired and discouraged. Keep your energy up. Balance your days. I was once on the road for an extended period of time, doing two or three sponsor sales meetings a day. In Tulsa, I had dinner with an old friend. She kept frowning at me as we chatted. I finally asked her what was wrong. She told me I looked exhausted. I glanced at my reflection in the window. She was right. My "scorched fields" approach to selling had taken its toll. This business of dashing through airports in high heels, eating bad food, and losing sleep was not fun; it was drudgery. I took myself off the road for awhile and restructured my sales approach, as well as my travel schedule. Life got easier. I started enjoying selling again and made more headway with less effort.

Finally, even when your program for seeking sponsorship is up and running and enjoyment comes more easily, you will want to continue to cultivate the behaviors discussed in this chapter for selling, negotiating, and closing the deal until they become routine and you can command profound results year after year.

Chapter 7

Understanding Sponsorship's Legal and Tax Concerns

NONPROFITS SEEKING SPONSORSHIPS often wonder if they will encounter legal or tax issues. Certainly, when a nonprofit enters a business relationship with a corporation it's a good idea to have a written agreement. And creating a solid written agreement that protects both sides is not as complicated as you might imagine. There are tax considerations as well, but they shouldn't impede your progress. The purpose of this chapter is to help you understand some of the legal and tax implications of sponsorship, which can be as severe as a loss of tax-exempt status or, far more commonly, the creation of taxable income. Understand that the information provided in this chapter is to make you aware of the fundamentals. It is neither exhaustive nor definitive. It is not intended to take the place of professional legal or accounting advice. Instead, use the material in this chapter to work more efficiently with lawyers and accountants to save your organization time and money.

The principal tax question raised by sponsorships is whether the payments to your exempt organization are subject to *unrelated business income tax* (UBIT). Payments received for advertising generally are taxable, whereas payments for which the sponsor or donor receives an acknowledgment are not taxable. With sponsorship the line is hard to draw. To help sponsees in structuring their arrangements, the IRS proposed regulations to implement this safe harbor in 1999. After seeking comments from the industry, the regulations were finalized, effective as of April 25, 2002, for sponsorship payments solicited or received after 1997. Despite having more regulations in place, the distinction between a sponsorship payment that is taxable and one that is not is still subject to interpretation. For your workaday purposes, it is necessary to know which sponsor rights and benefits will trigger UBIT.

Understanding the Basics

Defining the Qualified Sponsorship Payment

Under the new regulations there is a *safe harbor* for sponsor payments that qualify for tax exemption. These exempt payments are called *qualified sponsorship payments* (QSPs). Any payment made by a business where there is no "arrangement" or "expectation" that there will be a "substantial return benefit" for that payment is considered a QSP. The scope of sponsored activities that can qualify as exempt has been expanded. For instance, it is irrelevant whether the sponsored activity is related or unrelated to the organization's exempt purpose. Attorney LaVerne Woods, considers this "a key provision for events such as charity auctions, walk-a-thons, and other fundraising events that bear no direct relationship to exempt purposes, other than the need for funds" (Woods, 2002, p. 176). The sponsored activity may be a single event or an activity of continuing involvement that lasts an entire fiscal year or years. It is also irrelevant whether the sponsored activity is temporary or permanent, such as a permanent exhibition at a museum.

Defining Substantial Return Benefit

If qualifying for the safe harbor of the qualified sponsorship payment requires that there is no expectation the sponsor will receive a *substantial return benefit*, then it is important to determine what the IRS considers a substantial return benefit. The regulation defines it as any benefit other than (1) certain goods or services of insubstantial value or (2) a use or acknowledgment. Any advertising, as defined in the regulations, and any grant of an exclusive provider benefit, whereby the organization agrees that it will only allow the sale of the sponsor's product in connection with an activity in return for a fee to the organization, are considered substantial return benefits.

Defining Insubstantial Value

Certain goods and services are deemed *insubstantial* if their overall fair market value does not exceed 2 percent of the entire sponsor payment across an entire fiscal year.

Consider this example:

A pizza chain provides uniforms to players on a non-profit, amateur sports team, as well as funding for the team. The uniforms bear the pizza chain's name and logo. During a tournament, the organization distributes souvenir flags bearing the organization's name to employees of the pizza chain who come out to support the team. The value of the flags does not exceed 2% of the total value of the funding and uniforms provided by the pizza chain, and the flags, therefore, are not a substantial return benefit [Woods, 2002, p. 180].

In this example, Woods points out, the funding and uniforms provided by the pizza chain are a qualified sponsorship payment and not subject to UBIT.

Applying the Regulations to Your Sponsors' Benefits

The following guidelines are based on the typical rights and benefits that nonprofits offer to sponsors. This information will help you anticipate how the sponsor rights and benefits in your package might be construed by an auditor.

Use of Marks and Logos

Shared use of marks and logos or the nonprofit's acknowledgment of the sponsor's name or product lines is not considered a substantial return benefit, so it falls within the safe harbor. To keep your sponsor acknowledgments safe from UBIT you cannot include in an acknowledgment advertising for sponsor products or services that is qualitative or comparative or that supplies price information or other messages about savings or value, an endorsement, or an inducement to purchase, sell, or use the products or services. So, on the one hand, a payment to a nonprofit in exchange for the acknowledgment "Proudly sponsored by Mercedes Benz" is not taxable. On the other hand, a payment for the acknowledgment "Visit your Mercedes Benz dealer today, and test drive the new C-class, the official car of the Newport Jazz Festival," falls outside the safe harbor and the portion of the sponsor fees associated with that message will be subject to UBIT.

The acknowledgments that are allowable and considered qualified sponsor payments include

- Logos and slogans minus any qualitative or comparative descriptions of the sponsor's products, services, facilities, or company

- A qualitative message that is an established part of a company's official identity, such as, presumably, "Coca-Cola, Always Refreshing"

- A list of the locations, telephone numbers, or Internet addresses

- Value-neutral descriptions, including displays or visual depictions of the sponsor's goods or services
- The sponsor's brand or trade names and product or service listings

Sampling and Product Display

Sampling and *product display* fall within the safe harbor. The distribution of the sponsor's product at a sponsored activity, whether in the form of free samples or samples offered at a price, is not considered by the IRS as an inducement to purchase, sell, or use the sponsor's product. The same is true for product display, which would include placing a sponsor's vehicle in the lobby.

Hyperlinks

When the nonprofit organization allows Internet users to link from the nonprofit organization's Web site to the sponsor's Web site, the hyperlink will not by itself cause a sponsorship payment to be taxable.

Royalty Payments

Under the Internal Revenue Code, royalties are exempt from UBIT. This permits sponsors to use a nonprofit's name for a cause-marketing tie. When the relationship is structured so that the organization receives a royalty based on units sold bearing its name, the royalties paid out to the organization avoid taxation.

Red Flags

The following sponsor benefits are red flags for auditors. You may still want to offer some combinations of these benefits to sponsors. Just consider that the fees associated with them will likely be taxable.

Sponsor Exclusivity

Payments made in exchange for exclusive provider arrangements (for example, an official soft drink designation that includes exclusive pouring rights) fall outside the safe harbor and are likely subject to UBIT. This was a controversial position for the agency to take. Possibly to quell some of the anticipated outcry, the IRS commentary explains that such payments may still escape UBIT under other provisions of the tax law if available. Because exclusivity is a core benefit of most sponsorship programs, let's sift through the implications.

The important distinction here is that an exclusive *provider* arrangement does not qualify for the safe harbor, and the fee paid for this benefit would be subject to taxation. But an exclusive *sponsor* arrangement *that includes no additional rights to be the sole vendor or seller of a product at your facility or event* falls within the safe harbor. It will not fail because of its exclusivity. The IRS explains exclusivity as "an exclusive sponsor arrangement" where the sponsor receives the right to be the only sponsor of the event or activity or at least the only sponsor from a particular trade or industry. Understand, then, that acknowledgment of a sponsor as an exclusive sponsor is not by itself a substantial return benefit. This means that if a company receives as its only benefit an announcement that it is the exclusive sponsor of an event, there is no substantial return benefit and the sponsor's payment will not be subject to UBIT.

> A school district receives a substantial payment from a soft drink manufacturer. The district agrees to throw in the naming of a basketball tournament after the sponsor and also agrees to limit all soft drink sales through vending machines to the manufacturer's brand. The value of the exclusive provider part of the deal is worth more than 2 percent of the total payment to the district. The right to lock out soft drink competitors from selling in the schools is a substantial return benefit, and any payment will be taxable. Only the portion of the payment, if any, that the district can show exceeds the value of the exclusive provider arrangement is a qualified sponsor payment.

TIP

Because this regulation was so hotly debated, there is additional language in the preamble to the regulation that discusses exceptions and caveats. Although you should work with your own tax professional, it is safest to treat the fees associated with the exclusive provider benefit as taxable, along with the other red-flag benefits. In your record keeping, set a fair market value for these benefits in advance, so that you are paying UBIT only on that portion of the fees associated with the taxable benefit and are not being taxed on the total payment.

Advertising

The solicitation and receipt of fees from advertising in your organization's "regularly scheduled and printed material," such as a regular periodical, even if that publication serves an exempt purpose, constitutes a separate, unrelated trade or business, and so the net income from that advertising is taxable. For example, if a symphony orchestra makes a full-page ad in its monthly program booklet part of the sponsor's package, the ad revenue is taxable. What a nonprofit may be able to do is to have the sponsor pay for the direct expense of printing in return for acknowledgment in the publication. This may be considered a fair exchange, depending on how costs add up, and may move the advertising into the safe harbor. Use your judgment here.

Endorsements

There are no gray areas surrounding endorsements of a sponsor's product. It seems the IRS views endorsements as flagrant exploitation for commercial advantage of the goodwill and trust the nonprofit has built up with the public. An endorsement is considered a substantial return benefit. Be aware that the regulations do not elaborate on what constitutes an endorsement.

Database Usage

Payments received from the sale of your organization's database have often but not always been taxable. Whether you rent your list or sell it outright, the IRS may see this as a substantial return benefit with a definable fair market value. Be sure to review this with your tax professional if you are inclined to do it.

Guaranteed Exposure or Impressions

A payment that is tied to the degree of public exposure to an event or events, such as the level of attendance or broadcast ratings, falls outside the safe harbor and will be subject to UBIT. Likewise, fees earned in connection with a qualified convention or trade show activity, if your organization is an association, are not covered by the safe harbor.

Simple Rules of Thumb

You are not expected to be a lawyer or accountant when you set out to seek sponsors for your tax-exempt organization. So let's make it simple. The following principles should be kept in mind:

- A payment may be a qualified sponsorship payment whether the sponsored activity is related or unrelated to your organization's exempt purpose.

- The fact that a payment is contingent on the sponsored activities actually occurring will not by itself prevent the payment from being exempt.

- Printed material includes what is published electronically. This does not mean that every Web site is a periodical, however.

- If the 2 percent limit is exceeded, the entire value of the benefits to the sponsor, not merely the excess, is a substantial return benefit.

- Logos and slogans that are an established part of the sponsor's identity are safe.

- If the only benefit a sponsor receives is an announcement that it is the exclusive sponsor of an event, there is no substantial return benefit and the payment will be a QSP.

These new rules call for some thoughtful record keeping. One of the simplest things you can do is to consider your written sponsorship agreements to be important tax documents for your organization. File extra copies with your accounting department. Your organization's legal counsel will help you craft sponsor agreements in such a way as to avoid unnecessary confusion and UBIT. Consider also that if one of your sponsor payments falls outside the safe harbor, it does not mean that it is automatically taxable. Rather, the treatment of any payment continues to be determined under the existing UBIT rules. Ask your legal counsel to help you find ways, and they almost always exist, to structure your organization's sponsorship program to avoid UBIT.

Practice Guidelines

LaVerne Woods has generously provided the following guidelines to help your legal counsel and accountant work with the tax code:

- Exempt organizations should avoid use of qualitative or comparative terms and endorsements in acknowledging sponsors. A payment that is acknowledged only by: "Proudly sponsored by Joe's Coffee" is a nontaxable qualified sponsorship payment. A payment acknowledged by: "Proudly sponsored by Joe's Coffee, it's the best, try some" may be taxable advertising income.

- A sponsorship payment qualifies for the nontaxable safe harbor only to the extent that it exceeds the value of any benefits that the sponsor receives in return (such as dinners, tickets, and golfing opportunities). The burden is on the exempt organization to establish the value of any return benefits. Sponsorship agreements should specifically identify the value allocable to sponsor benefits, determined on a reasonable basis.

- Benefits that the exempt organization provides to the sponsor, the total value of which does not exceed 2% of the sponsor's payments, will be disregarded and will not affect the qualification of the sponsorship payment for the safe harbor. This 2% rule applies on an annual basis, which means that the relative values of sponsorship payments and benefits must be analyzed for each year of a multi-year sponsorship agreement.

- If the value of the benefits provided to the sponsor, such as advertising or an exclusive provider arrangement, exceeds 2% of the sponsor's payment, it may be preferable to separate out the benefit arrangement into another contract under which the sponsor pays fair market value for the benefit, with a corresponding reduction in the amount paid under the sponsorship agreement.

- If a sponsorship payment does not meet the safe harbor, there may be other avenues for avoiding tax. The activity producing the income may not be regularly carried on, or the income may constitute royalties (e.g., for use of the organization's logo or mailing list) or another category of income excluded from unrelated business income [Woods, 2002, pp. 186–187].

Written Agreements

The existence of a written sponsorship agreement, regardless of its detail, does not by itself exempt a sponsor payment from UBIT. However, having a solid written agreement upfront can save you the stress of untangling misunderstandings down the road. If you are quick to put forward your own contract, you may enjoy more control of the process. But don't be surprised if very large companies and their phalanxes of lawyers dismiss it. Corporate strictures around contracts can be such that another organization's insistence on its own contract is seen as a deal-breaker. If that becomes the case in your negotiations, it is better to proffer your contract as a guideline to help your organization and the sponsor draft a contract that both of you can sign off on quickly. What to call the document is another nuance. The term *contract*, because it sounds imposing, may slow verbal acceptance of the offer you are proposing. Instead, you might call the document a *memo of understanding* or a *letter of agreement*.

To further speed the process of gaining written agreement, use the following samples as a place to begin.

The Memo of Intent

The use of the memo of intent was introduced to me by Rob Prazmark, who sells the top tier of sponsorships for the Olympics. The main purpose of this memo is to lock the sponsor in while the details and final approvals are being worked out, but it has other uses as well. Sometimes the person you are negotiating with may not have full and final authority, which means you are not negotiating with the decision maker. This memo will flush that out, Prazmark advised me, because the recipient will need to seek approval to sign off. By floating a memo of intent you will learn who is actually aware of your arrangement and who is empowered to sign off on it. This tool is also helpful for getting a commitment from busy decision makers who want to lock into a deal with you but need more time to give full attention to the contract. Exhibit 7.1 contains a sample memo of intent.

The Written Sponsorship Agreement

Exhibit 7.2 is a *template* for a sponsorship agreement. It does not represent a particular negotiated contract; instead it suggests the areas many organizations will need to address. Use this template in consultation with a licensed, practicing attorney.

TIP

Do not make your proposal an official attachment to an agreement with a sponsor. The language of a proposal is designed to communicate the tangible, commercial benefits to the sponsor. By making it an attachment, you run the risk of exposing the entire sponsor payment to UBIT.

Specialized Legal Clauses

Certain issues crop up in sponsorship that inspire language that might be unfamiliar to you. The following discussions will help you interpret what's being said in regard to two of these issues.

EXHIBIT 7.1

Sample Memorandum of Intent

MEMORANDUM

TO: [*Decision Maker*], [*Company*]

FROM: [*Organization*]

DATE: [*Current date*]

RE: [*Company*] Sponsorship

This is to confirm that [*Company*] will be joining [*Organization*] as a sponsor of the _____
to be held during the _____ .

I will be following up with a formal agreement that details your rights and benefits as a sponsor. For now,
let this memo act as confirmation that [*Company*] will sponsor the _____ at the $_____
Presenting Sponsor level.

Please sign this memo and fax it back at your earliest convenience, so that we can reserve your package
of exclusive rights and benefits.

On behalf of [*Organization*], I thank you for your support and look forward to working with you.

_____   _____

[*Company*] Representative   Date

_____   _____

[*Organization*] Representative   Date

Morals Clauses

Morals clauses in sponsorship agreements grew out of their use in endorsement contracts with celebrities and athletes. They have been adopted by high-profile nonprofits to protect what is often their greatest asset: their reputation for doing good things. When entering into a relationship with a for-profit company, some nonprofits use a morals clause that allows termination of the relationship if the company engages in actions that create scandal and in turn do harm to the reputation of the nonprofit. Although having a morals clause in your contract will tell the sponsor that your organization takes the value of its name and reputation seriously, these clauses stick only when they describe the types of behaviors that apply. For example, the

EXHIBIT 7.2

Sample Sponsorship Agreement

This will confirm the terms and conditions on which [*Company*] ("You"/"Company") have agreed to sponsor the [*name of the event*] ("Event") organized by [*Organization*] ("Us"/"Organizer").

1. We shall use our best efforts to conduct and promote [*describe*].

2. We hereby grant you the right to be [an *or* the] official Sponsor of the Event.

3. We shall use our best efforts to provide you with [*describe the rights and benefits, including all the specifics (for example, how many signs and their dimensions and locations, number of pieces of collateral, where sponsor logo will be placed)*].

4. We shall provide you with _____ free tickets.

5. We shall give you credit as [a] sponsor in all advertising and promotional materials prepared by us, in the following form: "[*Company*], major sponsor of the *Event*."

6. If we produce a videotape of the Event for home distribution or broadcast or other use, we will use our best efforts to provide you with sponsorship credit therein.

7. In consideration of all rights granted you hereunder, you will pay us $_____, payable as follows:

    50% upon signing

    50% upon our delivery of a written final report to you

8. Company agrees to promote the Event in the following mutually agreed-upon ways:

    [List all promotions, including signage, TV, radio, and print.]

9. All correspondence, including payment, shall be sent to:

    [*Name*]

    [*Organization*]

    [*Mailing address*]

    [*Telephone*]

10. All uses of our trademarks and logos by Company and/or its advertisers are subject to our prior written approval. Company agrees to submit samples of all material using our trademarks and logos, including material produced by its advertisers, to us for approval, and we shall have fewer than seven (7) business days to approve or disapprove such material.

EXHIBIT 7.2

Sample Sponsorship Agreement, Cont'd

11. All uses of the trademarks and logos of Company by us are subject to Company's prior approval. We agree to submit samples of all material using Company's trademarks and logos, to Company for its approval, and Company shall have fewer than seven (7) business days to approve or disapprove such material.

12. Each party represents and warrants that it is free to enter into this Agreement without violating the rights of any person, that its trademarks do not infringe the trademarks or trade names of any person, and that it will comply with all laws and regulations pertinent to its business. You shall indemnify and hold us harmless from any liability arising out of the use of your products.

13. In the event that the Event does not take place due to any cause beyond the reasonable control of the parties, this Agreement shall terminate and our only obligation shall be to return to you the fee paid us hereunder less any direct out-of-pocket expenses incurred by us prior to the date of termination.

14. We shall not be held liable for any failure on the part of your employees or agents to deliver items or fulfill tasks such as [*list activities such as working the sponsor's display booth at the event or delivering samples to the event*].

15. This Agreement does not constitute a partnership or joint venture or principal agent relationship between us. This Agreement may not be assigned by either party. It shall be governed by the laws of the State of [*organization's home state*]. It is complete and represents the entire agreement between the parties.

If this accurately sets forth the Agreement between us and you, please sign below and return a copy to execute the Agreement.

_____

Executive Director, [*Organization*]

Agreed and accepted this _____ day of _____, 2003.

_____

Authorized [*Company*] Representative

Attachments:
Media schedule
Riders outlining paid, UBIT-related benefits such as advertising or booth space
Payment schedules

felony conviction of a member of the senior management at the sponsor company is a specific transgression that would clearly have an echoing impact on organizations affiliated with that company.

Force Majeure

The intent of the force majeure clause is to protect the sponsor's investment against calamity. It covers the unforeseeable and unpreventable, the "act of God" that can prevent an event from occurring or a personality from appearing. Some sponsors will want to outline a specific remedy if such an event occurs, such as a return or reduction of their fee.

A Word About Program Theft

The theft of a program concept can happen when sponsors and sponsees come together during the early development of a new event or program. Naturally the sponsor is in on the ground level and feels more ownership than the sponsor who becomes involved with an established event. As the event or program develops, the sponsor may want more input on content and management issues than your organization is willing to grant. To protect your organization from having the sponsor walk away with the event idea and replicate it at that point, thereby competing against you, Mary Hutchings Reed, my firm's lawyer and author of the *IEG Legal Guide to Sponsorship*, recommends that you build a few things into your agreement and program recipe:

- Spend time and effort developing the look of the program's identity and collaterals. Nonprofits often do this on the cheap to save money. Creating distinctive marks and logos not only helps you drive attendance and makes you more marketable, it helps you to protect your program legally from replication.

- Trademark or copyright, as appropriate, all the materials, descriptions, and names of things associated with the program.

- Include a noncompete clause in the agreement. Reed recommends the following language for your agreement:

  Sponsor represents and warrants that for a period of two years after the termination or expiration of this agreement it will not directly or indirectly conduct, sponsor, present, supply or otherwise be associated with an event substantively similar to [event name] anywhere in [specify region or country] [Reed, 1989, p. 181].

Conclusion

The tax and legal parameters of sponsorship are manageable. They shouldn't keep you from pursuing sponsorships. The key is to understand the potential sore spots and draft your agreements to address them upfront, so they never become an issue.

Chapter 8

Delivering the Deal and Communicating the Results

AT SOME POINT after taking all the proper steps you will be holding a signed sponsorship agreement. Now it's time to deliver. There is no secret sauce or metric formula for this work. It boils down to just two simple things: doing what the agreement promises and proving that it's been done. Interlacing the two is a steady stream of credible communication with the sponsoring company or its agents. That's it.

So if this work is so easy, why does this phase of the relationship seem so fraught with uncertainty? It is probably because the tools for "proving" that a nonprofit is delivering to a sponsor are still evolving. This chapter gives you practical aids to help you track your deals, along with simple advice. All the material in this chapter has been tested in the field and has worked. There are other approaches you can take. There are plenty of fancy marketing instruments you can consider, but they are costly. The plain truth is that quality properties deliver solid results not by spending on expensive measurement instruments but by keeping the sponsor informed throughout the fulfillment process so there are no surprises.

Getting Started Internally

The first steps involve preparing your organization to execute the agreement. Your organization will need to build an internal team to execute the agreement, a team that understands, and cares about, the alliance you have worked so hard to forge. Then the team will need to prepare means of tracking and measuring fulfillment.

Creating a Delivery System

Early in the process of seeking sponsorship, you will have received approval from the key players in your organization that empowered you to sell and negotiate. So there should be no surprises when you review the terms of the deal with your internal team.

The following action items will help you execute with ease:

Step 1. Send out a brief memo sharing the good news about the new sponsor you have recruited, and invite appropriate parties to attend the meeting. Attach an agenda. If you rely on others to deliver the deal, running meetings efficiently and making the best use of the team members' time and talents will yield stronger results.

Step 2. Walk the team through key sections of the written agreement. Invite questions and discussion as you go. Set up a quarterly meeting schedule, monthly if the relationship with the sponsor is more demanding.

Step 3. Assign a person to take meeting minutes. (Worksheet 8.1 is a tool for this process.) Distribute copies after each meeting, and make copies available at future meetings. In my experience, frequent documentation and follow-up with the team binds people to shared outcomes.

WORKSHEET 8.1

Minute Minder

Use the following chart to take minutes at team meetings. Distribute copies of these minutes so that each team member has an actionable record of the decisions made and the person responsible for carrying out each action.

Item	Gist of Discussion	Action Required	Person Responsible	Due Date

Becoming the Sponsor's Advocate

A shift occurs once a deal is done. You will go from being your organization's advocate to being the sponsor's advocate. This will seem puzzling to your colleagues. "Whose side are you on anyway?" you may hear. Remember, your transformation to sponsorship marketer is complete only when you have sold, negotiated, closed, and *delivered*. Your sense of obligation to the sponsor will put you in the position of having to argue the sponsor's case to the internal audience. To facilitate better understanding, provide your team with as much information about the sponsor, the sponsor's culture, and the terms of the deal as possible.

Defining Roles: Who Does What?

Plan a kickoff meeting with the sponsor's team. Invite your team along if the execution of the relationship is heavily detail oriented and the sponsor's team is expected to share duties with your team. For instance, as part of a sponsorship deal between a national children's cause and a major computer hardware company, the cash fee was reduced in exchange for services from the sponsor's public relations department. With four major events planned, several waves of media relations had to be staged. The cause had a tiny public relations department but a senior-level executive to oversee the effort. It was essential to have the corporate public relations director and that nonprofit executive walk through the promotional schedule together, discuss the approvals process, and hash out the what-if scenarios.

Staying Organized: Punch Lists for Your Staff

A list of the practical aspects of what it will take to deliver can be taken directly from the sponsorship agreement. Use this list with your team to walk through the aspects of fulfillment. It should become the central punch list for who does what. It is also important that this list notes what needs to be photographed or monitored for your organization's final report to the sponsor. The specific items covered will depend on your property. Worksheet 8.2 will give you some ideas. Adapt it as necessary to fit your property.

Building In Measurement

There are marketing tactics you can build into your program that automatically trigger measurable results. I have been inspired by the sponsorship

WORKSHEET 8.2

What It Will Take to Deliver on the Agreement

Write in the answer to each question in the space provided. Adapt categories and questions as necessary to fit your property.

Sponsor Status

1. What is the official status (title sponsor, presenting sponsor, cosponsor), and what is included?

2. Is the status year-round or just for this event?

3. Is the status for just this venue or program or across the organization?

4. Notes:

Signage

1. Where will signage be placed?

2. What size is it?

3. Do we produce it or does the sponsor?

4. Is any additional labor or construction required to install it? Sponsor's crew or ours?

5. Who pays for labor and materials?

6. What is the approval process?

7. Should it be photographed?   _____ Yes   _____ No

8. Notes:

WORKSHEET 8.2, Cont'd

On-Site Selling

1. What products will be sold?

2. Are there conflicts with any existing vendors?

3. Will sponsor have its own sales booth or tent?

4. Selling logistics: how is product delivered? who will sell and take money? is a cash register needed? if so, who pays?

5. Should it be photographed? _____ Yes   _____ No

6. Notes:

Sponsor Payment

1. Review payment schedule.

2. Will activity begin only with deposit or begin immediately?

3. What deliverables are required for payment?

4. Notes:

Sampling or Product Display

1. When will samples or products be delivered?

2. What are the space and security requirements?

3. Should it be photographed? _____ Yes   _____ No

4. Notes:

WORKSHEET 8.2, Cont'd

Unpaid Media (PR)

1. Review public relations schedule.

2. Review sponsor boilerplate.

3. What is the approval process?

4. Who handles questions from the media? Who is the official spokesperson?

5. Who develops key talking points on the relationship?

6. Who produces and places public service announcements or B-rolls?

7. Hire a clipping service?   _____ Yes   _____ No

8. Notes:

Paid Media

1. What is guaranteed: programs? brochures? posters? shared advertising buys?

2. Is there any television or videotaping? Are there postproduction spots or billboards?

3. Should media be photographed?   _____ Yes   _____ No

4. Notes:

VIP/Hospitality

1. Are these any special setups, private spaces, tent?

2. Who does the inviting?

3. Where will celebrity meet-and-greets occur? Any restrictions?

WORKSHEET 8.2, Cont'd

4. Is the organization's board invited?

5. Are other sponsors invited? Any competitor issues?

6. Is catering expected? If so, who pays?

7. Should it be photographed?   _____ Yes   _____ No

8. Notes:

Mailings

1. Review database usage and logistics.

2. Review insertion mailing production schedule.

3. How will returned mail be handled?

4. Notes:

Day-to-Day Contact

1. Who is the primary point person on each side?

2. What is the expected medium for interaction: e-mail? phone? fax? Frequency?

3. Will an e-mail listserv be set up for the teams?

4. Notes:

executives who continually experiment with such tactics. New approaches emerge all the time, so it pays to keep in touch with colleagues in the field. Here are a few of the tried-and-true tactics:

Product trial and bounce-back tracking and reporting. Some sponsors distribute coupons or use some form of bounce-back device that can then be counted when redeemed. For example, a participant might be able to redeem a ticket stub for free or discounted products.

Sampling distribution. Sponsors who ask you to handle product sampling will have a specific number of samples shipped to you or delivered by representatives at the event. If all the samples are handed out, this becomes a measurable data point.

Sales receipts. Some sponsors will ask that you handle the sales of their products on-site. You will want to monitor and report on how many cases or units were delivered, how many were sold, and how many returned. Also include in the sales report the cost of making the sales and the revenue due to you. For instance, the Milwaukee Irish Festival has an arrangement with a beer company that allows it to add ten cents to every can of beer sold by festival volunteers. That's five cents to lift the can out of the ice, and five to hand it to the customer.

Database building. Sponsors often want to follow up with your audience with a direct-mail campaign. To generate a database they can have more access to than your membership database, they may build in an incentive such as a sweepstakes. (By the way, sweepstakes are regulated by their own body of law, so be sure to check with your lawyer if you plan to run one.) Again, the number of names they capture creates a measure of return on investment (ROI). Be careful to stipulate that any database the sponsor creates through your event is for the sponsor's sole use. There have been cases in which sponsors have sold names from such databases to other companies.

Exit surveys. These are helpful for you as well as your sponsors. Exit surveys help you gather plenty of information about how people experienced your event. You can even invite top-level sponsors to add a question to the survey and report the results back to them for further ROI. A key question to ask your participants is whether they can name the sponsors of the event. High sponsor recall is a slam dunk. Not only will your current sponsors appreciate the research, you can use this result as a testimonial to the power of your property in your sales materials. If you can afford to hire a third party to handle the survey process, all the better. Sponsors place a higher value on measurement particularly likely to be objective.

TIP

Be creative about tracking user passion for your event. For example, the International Olympic Committee and Visa, a top-tier Olympics sponsor, saw that schoolchildren were taking up the International Olympics theme in their artwork. Visa decided to build an entire program around this, with local competitions managed by its network of local banks. The program made the Olympics real to children worldwide; it was especially effective because art overcomes language barriers. The IOC and Visa saw the program as tangible evidence of the international power of the games as a cultural phenomenon.

Ongoing Interaction with the Sponsor

Over the period of the sponsorship, you should plan on interacting with sponsors to keep them informed and also interested in your organization beyond the deal itself. It may also be necessary to actively cope with cultural clashes between your organization and the sponsor's company and any sponsor dissatisfaction that surfaces as your event or program is carried out.

Structuring Communications to Keep Sponsors Coming Back

To maintain ongoing communication with sponsors, take steps to create an information loop. Make sure they are on the general mailing list. Invite them to informal and formal gatherings and events, even if these are not a part of their sponsorship package. Encourage cross-promotions and business ties among your sponsors; it will help to keep them loyal. For example, invite them to the sponsor recruitment business breakfast or set up a separate event hosted by a board member where sponsors can talk about their tie-ins and explore cross-promotions.

The National Park Service's Proud Partners of America's National Parks sponsorship program holds an annual partner conference to share consumer leisure trends tracked by the parks, forecasts about programs under development, and an overall report of what the parks delivered for sponsors in the previous year. "We attend every year because it gives us a chance to connect with other partners and build strong and productive relationships. Obviously, we share values and business interests with the other sponsors, so it's easy to get conversations going," reports Carrie Passmore (2003), SVP, Public Partnerships for Discovery Communications, including Discovery's media sponsorship with the parks.

Dealing with a Culture Clash

If your sponsorship project is big enough or complex enough, a sponsorship deal can feel like a minimerger. Cultures can collide, as this case study illustrates.

> A national education cause that was headed up by a group of passionately committed Ph.D.'s arranged a sponsorship deal with a well-known packaged goods brand with a sterling reputation. However, the new marketing director for the brand had come out of sports marketing. She brought with her a boutique marketing agency that focused on managing sports ties and athlete endorsements. The negotiations had gone well, but when it came time to execute the agreement, the sponsor's brand manager handed the project off to this agency.
>
> The culture clash began. The agency was unsympathetic to the organization's policies and procedures and continually sought to negotiate added benefits, above and beyond the agreement. Its staff e-mailed requests to the nonprofit, expecting immediate turnaround. The sponsee stonewalled, offering no alternatives or suggestions for accomplishing the same objectives in ways acceptable to it.
>
> The agency became combative. The sponsee went back to the sponsor and pleaded for relief. Finger pointing ensued. Each side ended up resenting the other and completed each phase of the rollout with repressed hostility. The marketing manager wondered why the deal never really played out the way she expected. There wasn't any juice or synergy left in the relationship. Both sponsor and sponsee felt used and unhappy.

There are some lessons here.

It is best not to assume that the people you are negotiating with and have probably come to feel comfortable with will be managing the execution of the deal. Even if there is no agency at the table during the negotiation, don't assume there isn't one in the wings. The bigger the company the more likely it is to ask an agency to execute the deal. Ask beforehand who will be on the implementation team. If an agency will be involved, plan on meeting with agency staff as soon as the deal is finalized to establish roles and goals for working together.

However, don't invite the agency in during the negotiations unless you suspect it can be helpful in some way. Marketing agencies rarely are at this stage. It is their job to protect their client and increase their billables. They can be hardboiled negotiators and arrogant collaborators. Know this and find appropriate ways to work with them, such as gaining approvals for collaterals, seeking advice on added-value opportunities that come up, and working out project timetables. Their goal is to demonstrate their value to the client, so the more gems you hand them to pass on to the client, the more they will support you.

Finally, always be pleasant, even when you have to be firm. This applies to dealing with both agencies and sponsors of course. I learned this the hard way. By mistaking my organization's assets for my own, I became overly protective. I forgot that in the end the executive was just doing his job. It's business, not personal. By losing my temper I proved only one thing: I was good at getting mad. That's fruitless.

Handling Dissatisfaction

If the sponsor is having a less than satisfactory experience, you are likely to hear about it quickly, and you should try to remedy the situation as promptly as possible. Even if your solutions resolve the sponsor's problems, expect those problems to come up again in the final report and renewal-seeking phase as a point for negotiation. If there has been serious breach of the agreement, it will be very difficult to mend the relationship, even with a good final reporting process or through renewal negotiations. Salvaging broken trust is next to impossible.

If the breach was caused by your organization's lack of delivery on some key aspect, you should take responsibility right away. Begin creating a paper trail of memos regarding what happened and the remedies, or *make-goods*, you are offering. These memos may become legal documents. Be careful not to open the door to outrageous requests to make good. Come forward with the makegood package and be clear about your limitations as well as your regrets that the deal went off track. If the sponsor refuses to negotiate and wants cash back or to withhold payment, you should call your attorney for advice, and in many cases it is wise to halt further fulfillment until you and the sponsor have agreed on how to proceed.

Your contract should have a force majeure clause that covers acts of God, which means any situation beyond your control, such as weather, injured or no-show celebrities, and so forth. If there has been a material breach on your part, expect to lose a portion of the sponsorship fee.

If the sponsor's dissatisfaction arises from a misunderstanding rather than an outright failure on your organization's part, understand that the most common reason misunderstandings occur is that the sponsor was imagining one thing and got another. Sometimes this happens because the sponsor failed to articulate an objective. Once, when my firm was working with a sponsor who was new to sponsorship and had sent the sponsor's decision maker a follow-up outline of all the rights and benefits he should seek to negotiate from the property, he asked why a certain copromotion wasn't on the list. It was something we had discussed in a brainstorming session, but he made no indication at the time that it was a critical element. However, as I teased out his thoughts I realized he had spent a lot of time picturing this event in his head.

After an event or program unfolds, the sponsor can feel a bit deflated if the reality doesn't measure up to what had been imagined, but this need not translate into dissatisfaction. If the sponsor is provided with enough positive results, plus any serendipitous outcomes that were achieved, then any misunderstanding is quickly overshadowed. The way you reinforce these positive results is with a final report. This report allows you to tell the story of what the alliance achieved so that the sponsor can replace any uncertainties or concerns over unmet expectations with the pleasure of seeing real results.

Reporting Results: The Final Analysis

Final reports can be simple or elaborate. The more a sponsor has paid for the alliance, the greater the expectation will be of a report with plenty of measured data points that help the sponsor gauge return on investment. Some nonprofits prepare CD-ROM reports that include video clips of the event along with exit survey comments obtained by third-party researchers from attendees. If your budget is limited, a written report with a scrapbooklike binder will work too. This binder might include, for example, all the event collaterals, copies of any news articles, and a one-page sheet with data about attendance and the number of members exposed to the sponsor's identity as a result of the deal.

Final reports should contain the following:

- A narrative describing the project and its outcomes (1,000 to 1,500 words)

- Photos of the sponsor's signage in context of the event

- Results of any on-site or postevent surveys, tabulated and distilled
- Media clippings
- A list of all media that covered the event
- A list of all cosponsors
- A direct-mail report, with drop dates and number of pieces returned

Present your final report in person if at all possible. If your contact at the company is out of town, you might consider a conference call, but face-to-face contact is always the most effective. Expect the meeting to take at least an hour. If you are confident the results are impressive, encourage your contact to invite other team members. Give a well-rounded report—share all the good news, but don't be afraid to expose some warts either. This will increase your credibility. And expect some criticism from the sponsor's team. A final report that does not call forth any criticism from the sponsor is actually a bad sign. It can mean the sponsor is less likely to renew. Why waste time reviewing an alliance that will not be in next year's portfolio?

Seeking Renewals

When you present each sponsor with a final report, you can use this face-to-face meeting to obtain a renewal or at least restart negotiations for those agreements that are not multiyear deals. This can be particularly important for your top tier of sponsors. Simply finish the presentation of results with a series of simple questions. For example, you might ask these questions, listening carefully to each answer:

"From our perspective, this seemed to work very well. What did you think?"

"Going forward, what would you do differently? How else could we be working with you?"

"We would like to begin thinking and planning for next year, in order to give your needs maximum consideration. Can we count you in again for next year?"

The seeds of every renewing sponsorship are planted in the delivery phase. A happy sponsor renews unless there are circumstances beyond his or her control. I once had a sponsor renew every year for five years, stopping only when the company was sold. Every other year the marketing contact changed, the company reorganized, and budget considerations were revisited, but the deal got funded each time. Why? Because the nonprofit documented every success, delivered reports that made everyone associated with the project feel accomplished, and forewarned the sponsor when things looked uncertain.

Not every sponsor you work with will be a match made in heaven. Some deals hit rough spots but over the long haul deliver nicely for both sides. Others step off on shaky footing and stay that way. Some are dream deals from the start and exceed everyone's wildest expectations. Whichever way your relationships unfold, keep in mind that friction commonly arises because one or both of the parties have envisioned some outcome beyond what is detailed in the contract, and the reality has not measured up to the vision. Understand, too, that sponsors take on considerable risk when they sign deals that are in some way nontraditional. In these cases sponsors can become hypervigilant for any signs of trouble, and your organization and the sponsor will quickly burn through the honeymoon phase.

By now you know sponsor relationships should be handled with care. Do your best to keep the communication flowing and expectations out in the open. Because your goal is to build a successful program, you will want to protect your reputation. That reputation, good or bad, will soon spread beyond your immediate sponsors as the marketing executives you have worked with migrate to other companies (and take good nonprofit partners with them).

Making a Long-Term Commitment to Sponsorship

All told it is not that hard to do a sponsorship deal. It is much harder to build a sustainable sponsorship program. Sadly, many organizations give up before they reach this point. The organizations that become powerhouses in building high-yield sponsorship programs do so because they understand one singular truth: it takes time to build anything of value. Anyone can do one deal. Serious players are able to do several, year after year.

The procedures I have described require a lot of work from you. But you are building equity in a program that will have long-term impact. Once you take the steps outlined in this book to grow your sponsorship program, your organization will be more visible and more successful at attracting people to its cause. Your work will become easier. Prospects will take your calls, and doors will start opening. You will generate momentum. You will have made the transition this book is all about. Away you go!

Glossary

BECAUSE MANY OF THE PEOPLE who negotiate sponsorships also work with other types of media, you may encounter the following terms in your work. This glossary will help you speak their language.

ADI Abbreviation for *area of dominant influence*. A geographical market area defined by a preponderance of radio listening. An ADI is analogous to a *DMA* and an *SMSA*, but may not be identical in area or size to these other market measuring devices. This term is now rarely used.

adjacency A position between two programs for a commercial. Applies to both radio and TV.

advertising agency An organization that prepares advertising materials for client organizations and that usually (but not always) also plans and buys advertising time or space for those clients. See also **buying service, media management service.**

advertising weight The level of advertising support provided to a brand, product, or service, expressed in terms of gross impressions, gross rating points, target rating points, number of insertions, and so forth.

affidavit Part of proof of performance; a statement supplied by both TV and radio media telling the advertiser the date and time at which the advertiser's commercial aired. See also **tearsheet.**

ARB Abbreviation for *Arbitron.* Arbitron asks a sampling of households to keep a diary in order to accumulate data on radio use and to provide ratings on audience size and composition.

Many of the media terms in this glossary were excerpted with permission from the Kelly, Scott & Madison *Glossary of Media Terms*, courtesy of the media marketing company of Kelly, Scott & Madison, Chicago, Illinois.

audience accumulation (CUME) The total audience, over time, for an advertising campaign. CUME represents the unduplicated reach of a campaign.

average frequency The average number of times any one person might have been exposed to a message during a specific time span. It is calculated by adding up impressions or exposures over a specific span of time, then dividing that sum by target audience size. Clearly, some targets will have seen, heard, or read the message more and some less than average. Average frequency can be calculated for any known target size. It can be calculated for one medium or a combination of media.

B2B (also **B-to-B**) Abbreviation for *business-to business* (advertising, sales, and so forth). Often used to describe e-commerce in which business vendor and business client use the Web to conduct their transaction.

B2C (also **B-2-C**) Abbreviation for *business-to-consumer*. Often used to describe e-commerce in which an on-line business and an individual consumer use the Web to conduct their transaction.

back-of-book That portion of a magazine behind the main editorial center section (or *editorial well*) banner. A Web advertisement served to a participating Web site's homepage. A banner is about one inch high by five inches long and typically runs across the top of the viewer's monitor. May also refer to street signage or event signage.

barter The exchange of advertising time or space in return for merchandise, services, or programming. Synonym: **trade** or **payment-in-kind.**

billboard (1) An announcement, typically five to ten seconds in length, identifying a sponsor at the beginning (*opening billboard*) or end (*closing billboard*) of a TV or radio program. (2) An old term for what is now called an *outdoor poster* or *outdoor display.*

bleed The use of the space that would normally be the empty margin around a print advertisement for the live matter of the ad itself. If you want your advertisement to fill the whole page including the margin, you pay extra—a *bleed charge.*

bonus spot A free announcement added to a TV or radio schedule—done to compensate for missed spots or other scheduling problems or to court the favor of an advertiser.

bookends The first and last positions in a TV commercial pod. Most likely to be called *bookends* when a single advertiser buys both positions for identical fifteen-second commercials.

bounce-back coupon A redeemable offer that "bounces" the customer back to the retailer or manufacturer to make a discounted purchase. These are often printed on the backs of tickets or other event collateral: for example, "Show this ticket and receive a free cup of coffee with your bagel purchase." It is considered to have greater value than simply printing the sponsoring company's name or logo on the collateral, as it triggers a purchase and creates a way to measure effectiveness of a sponsorship deal.

brand development index (BDI) A number representing a product's geographical sales strength or weakness derived from its sales compared to total sales to a target market. The geographical area may be of any size but is most commonly a DMA, SMSA, or other marketing unit. See also **category development index.**

buying service An organization specializing in the purchase of advertising time and space for advertisers or agencies. In contrast to media management services or advertising agencies, buying services typically provide no planning or production functions, although some may assist in traffic functions. See also **media management service, advertising agency.**

campaign Typically the total advertising effort on behalf of a brand, product, or service, within a predetermined timeframe and usually having a well-defined and limited number of advertising and marketing objectives.

cancellation date The final date for canceling any previously ordered media. See also **extension.**

category development index (CDI) A number representing a product's geographical strength or weakness based upon sales comparisons with respect to a particular product or service category. See also **brand development index.**

cause marketing A type of sponsorship in which the sponsor promotes its relationship with a charity, cause, or influential nonprofit to stimulate the purchase of products, and for each purchase a percentage donation is made to the cause.

circulation (circ.) The number of copies sold of any specific issue of a consumer magazine or newspaper. It includes both subscription copies delivered and individual newsstand sales. Circulation may also refer to other readership and production data that can be gleaned from circulation statements.

closing date The final date for contracting to run an ad in a newspaper or magazine. See also **extension.**

clutter High levels of sponsor messages and logos aggregated around one event or in one concentrated area.

combination rate A form of discount designed to encourage the use of two or more individual vehicles for a particular commercial or print advertisement.

competitive analysis Examination of advertising levels and scheduling patterns for competing brands, products, or services. Typically done with the use of secondary research resources provided by major monitoring organizations such as LNA, Strategy, and so on.

continuity (1) Maintenance of a regular and unbroken schedule of advertising (as in a campaign). (2) The production *book* of a radio or TV station. The *content* of broadcast or cable communication.

contract rate Typically used in newspaper advertising: special low rates earned by advertisers who sign annual contracts for newspaper advertising linage. Contract rates are published, not negotiated, rates. See also **short rate.**

cooperative advertising (co-op) The sharing of advertising media costs (and occasionally production costs) between a manufacturer or distributor and a downstream buyer and seller of merchandise or services.

corporate discount A reduction on the costs for individual ads or commercials, or a rebate of monies spent, based on overall spending and discounts thereby earned or negotiated by an organization.

cost efficiency A measure of media effectiveness based on a comparison of potential or actual audience and the cost of ad placement, usually expressed as cost-per-thousand households or cost-per-thousand persons, or cost-per-target demographic, and so forth.

cost-per-thousand (CPM, cpm) The cost of exposing an advertising message to 1,000 viewers, readers, or other target audience members, calculated by dividing total cost by total audience (in thousands). CPM is a basic measure of media efficiency; the typical fundamental comparison between competing media.

coverage (1) An advertising vehicle's reach expressed as a percentage of the total potential audience in a market. (2) An advertising vehicle's reach expressed as a percentage of a geographical region.

coverage map A map showing the effective reception area for a broadcast station's signal or the geographical reach of a print advertising vehicle. In the latter case it may present zip code analyses of newspaper and direct-mail circulation characteristics.

credit A financial adjustment for a missed advertising spot or sponsor benefit. See also **makegood.**

CUME See **audience accumulation.**

cut-in A locally aired TV commercial replacing a network-originated announcement *for the same advertiser.* Cut-ins command a premium cost but are often used to test copy, special offers, and the like.

data mining The analysis of information stored in a database to find significant patterns of thought, behavior, spending, and so forth, that might be of use to a marketer in furtherance of a marketing or advertising plan.

daypart Period of the broadcast day. For TV, the dayparts are *morning news, daytime early, fringe, early news, prime access, primetime, late news, late fringe, overnight.* For radio, typical dayparts are *morning drivetime* (or *AM drive*), *midday, afternoon drivetime* (or *PM drive*), *evening, overnight.* For network-affiliated TV and radio stations, *daytime* usually refers to the time period from 9:00 A.M. to 3:00 P.M. For independents it usually means the period from 6:00 A.M. to 3:00 P.M.

deal The sponsorship offer. Most commonly used when an offer has been accepted and transacted.

defensive spending An advertising budget strategy in which more advertising weight is given to geographical areas of current marketing strength. Designed to prevent inroads into a market by competition.

demographics The characteristics that define population segment. Typical characteristics important to marketers are age, sex, income, education, marital status, home ownership, family size, and the like. Demographics do not usually include so-called lifestyle characteristics. See also **PRIZM, VALS, psychographics.**

direct mail (DM) Mailings, typically to purchased lists of specific names but also to specific zip codes, encouraging a response to the mailed offer.

direct response (DR) Any advertising communication that encourages the target to use a feedback mechanism to respond to the message. This mechanism may be using a phone, reply card, FAX, or computer connection or writing a letter, and so forth.

discrepancy An unreconciled difference among station logs, contracts, invoices, and the media buyer's records.

DMA Abbreviation for *designated market area,* one of A. C. Nielsen's geographically defined TV markets. Analogous to, but not identical to, ADI and SMSA. This designation has replaced the ADI designation.

drop zone The zip code area, or publication *zone* area, for direct mail or freestanding insert advertising.

duplication (1) That portion of a medium's readers, listeners, or viewers shared with other media. See also **exclusive CUME.** (2) That portion of viewers seeing the same outdoor display board repeatedly, due to regular driving patterns.

earned rate The actual rate paid for print space, taking into account any volume discounts and frequency discounts. In some cases, for some advertisers and campaigns, adding funds for "extra" advertising can result in discounts easily exceeding the amount of money added.

editorial environment The perceived standards, content, tone, and philosophy of a medium. This is a subjective evaluation.

effective frequency The advertising frequency that meets some objective in the marketing plan. It can be evaluated for the total market or for a target population. It can also be evaluated for brand awareness, propensity to purchase, perceived satisfaction, and so forth. Effective frequency is almost always evaluated in combination with *effective reach.*

effective reach The advertising reach that meets some objective in the marketing plan. It indicates that sufficient readers, viewers, or listeners have seen or heard an advertising communication at some effective frequency. Effective reach is almost always evaluated in combination with *effective frequency.*

enhanced underwriting Sponsorship of a public broadcast program that includes a mention of the sponsor at the beginning and end of the program, plus one or more actual commercial positions adjacent to or within the program.

estimate (1) A summary of anticipated costs for a proposed advertising purchase. (2) A projection of possible audience size for a specific communications vehicle.

ethnic media Media targeted to U.S. demographic groups characterized by minority race, national background, cultural practices, or language. Examples are African American magazines, Hispanic TV, Polish newspapers, and Haitian radio.

exclusive CUME ARB measurement of listener loyalty. People who listen solely or almost solely to one radio station fall into this category.

exclusivity The purchased right to lock out other competitors in the sponsor's business category. When the sponsoring company buys the exlusive right to sell its product onsite or to be the sole vendor to the sponsee or its constituents as part of the overall sponsorship agreement, the fee associated with this form of exclusivity will be subject to taxation (UBIT) by the IRS.

exposure The presentation of a single advertisement or commercial to a single potential target. Note that exposure alone does not necessarily mean that target has seen, read, or understood the message.

extension (1) For periodicals, the time between the materials closing date and the final date for delivery of materials to the printer. (2) For broadcast media, the continuation of an existing advertising campaign for a specific period of time beyond its original contract date for completion.

e-zine A magazine published on the Web.

FCC Abbreviation for *Federal Communications Commission,* the agency regulating the use of the broadcast spectrum. It cooperates with regulatory bodies of other countries to prevent overlapping use and misuse of the broadcast spectrum.

flighting Scheduling alternating periods of activity (*flights*) and inactivity (*hiatuses*) on a TV or radio schedule. This strategy is typically used to spread out the commercials allowed by a limited advertising budget.

franchise position A specific position in a newspaper or magazine reserved for a particular advertiser. Some franchise positions are reserved by contract. Some are available to certain advertisers or advertising categories by tradition. Others are courtesies to large and consistent advertisers.

freestanding insert (FSI) A preprinted advertising message inserted into a fold of a newspaper, especially popular in Sunday editions. FSIs run from a single, two-sided leaf all the way up to a brochure or substantial catalogue.

frequency Number of exposures: that is, number of times an ad or commercial has been run. Note that frequency does not tell you whether the target has seen, read, or understood the advertising message.

frequency discount Reduced rates offered for multiple uses of a vehicle. The term is usually used in relation to printed vehicles.

frequency distribution A breakdown (graphical, preferably, or tabular) of the number of times various audience subgroups have been exposed to an ad.

FSI See **freestanding insert.**

gross (1) The cash amount a medium asks for its wares, exclusive of any discounts or other adjustments. See also **net.** (2) The total audience number, unadjusted for factors that might be important to the advertiser such as age, sex, and family size. See also **gross impressions.**

gross impressions The total number of exposures to an advertisement or commercial.

gross rating points (GRPs) Accumulated rating points, the basic advertising planning units. Calculated by multiplying reach times frequency. See also **target rating points.**

HDTV Abbreviation for *high-definition television,* a technical specification that results in extremely lifelike pictures being broadcast or cabled to viewers with the appropriate receiving equipment.

hiatus Period of time in an advertising campaign during which advertisements or commercials are not scheduled. See also **flighting.**

higher rate advertiser An advertiser willing to spend more than you do for the radio or TV positions for which you have contracted.

hit One response click on one hypertext word on one Web page by one online user. Hit may be thought of as analogous to an exposure.

hospitality package The use of a sponsored event to entertain the sponsor's clients. This is a common benefit found in sponsorship packages, in which special seating, complimentary tickets, and backstage or insider experiences are made available only to sponsors of the event.

hypertext A format for Web-site words or graphics that allows them to function as links to other Web locations; a click on specific hypertext moves the user to the linked location.

hybrid deal A sponsorship arrangement that supplies both philanthropic gifts or grants and marketing dollars, the latter added to promote the program funded by the gift.

ID Abbreviation for *identity,* such as a sponsor's name or logo placed on signage or in ten-second radio or TV tags.

impression One exposure in one household to one individual of one advertisement. Used interchangeably with *exposure.*

inch rate The cost of one column inch of space in a newspaper, used to compute newspaper advertising rates. A column inch is one inch long and one column wide (column width will vary from newspaper to newspaper).

Internet (Net) A complex, international matrix of connected computers and computer networks. The backbone network for the GUI-based (graphical user interface–based) Web.

interstitial A Web pop-up window containing advertising. Interstitials pop up as Internet pages are loading; in effect they appear in the interstices between loaded pages. Users have to click on them to close them.

intranet A network with restricted access. Typically, the authorized users are members of a single organization, and the network uses the Web interface of browser and http protocol. An intranet isolates itself from the Internet by using firewalls or by limiting the cabling used in the network installation.

inventory Unsold TV or radio station time that is available for sale to advertisers.

link A word or graphic that can be clicked to take the user to other locations on the Web site currently in use or on other Web sites. See also **hypertext.**

makegood Replacement of an advertising spot (or other scheduled item) that did not appear at all or was misscheduled with a spot (or other item) of equal or better value. See also **credit.**

media management service A business providing a full range of media-specific functions such as media planning, buying, and analysis. Media services typically do not provide production services for print, radio, or TV advertising. See also **buying service, advertising agency.**

Mediamark Research Inc. (MRI) A research organization measuring audience characteristics of various media, especially magazines, and providing cross-tabulations of product usage. See also **Simmons.**

media metrix The latest trade jargon for *media measurements.* (Singular: *media metric.*)

Media Metrics Meters actual usage of Web sites, on-line services, computer hardware, and other interactive applications. The sample consists of both home and work users. Two meters are used. Real-time tracking software monitors all Web activity of panel members. The *clickstream* data are sent back via the Web in real time. Other tracking software captures clickstream data on disk, and the disks are sent via mail for processing.

Media Networks, Inc. (MNI) A service for purchasing ad space in certain national magazines on a market-by-market basis. The ad size must be a page, B&W or color. Advertisers can have their ads delivered to the subscription audiences of a number of similar magazines, in zip-code specific areas, in 150 markets. For example, The News Network magazine package includes *Newsweek, Sports Illustrated, Time,* and *U.S. News & World Report.*

media planning The process of analyzing media and marketing information and designing schedules to meet specific advertising and marketing objectives.

medium Any vehicle used to deliver an advertising message. (Plural: *media.*)

mention (1) The portion of a commercial that gives a local retailer's name, address, phone, and so on. (2) The giving of credit in a TV or radio program to a product or service, in return for cash or payment in kind. (3) Shorthand for *product mention.*

metro area The central metropolitan core of a market, equivalent to the *standard metropolitan statistical area* (SMSA), defined by the U.S. government.

minimum frequency The minimum number of exposures thought necessary (or tested and proven necessary) for an advertisement to be effective, to have its planned result. In practice the minimum frequency is a rather elastic number. See also **effective frequency.**

monitor To check the appearance, time, and length of broadcast commercials and the appearance and unit size of print advertisements.

negotiation The give-and-take discussions regarding rates, position, promotional considerations, and other factors before an agreement to purchase advertising is finalized.

Nielsen NetRatings A service that collects Web use and advertising measurement information by tracking real-time Web-site and Web-advertising activity of a home-based sample and work panel sample. Tracking software monitors all Web activity of panel members. Clickstream data are sent back via the Web in real time.

net The dollar amount an advertising agency pays a medium for its wares. The net cost is less than the gross cost. The agency keeps the difference (typically 15 percent) between gross and net as its payment for services performed.

Nielsen Short form of *A. C. Nielsen Company,* a marketing and media research company that measures national and local TV viewing among a statistical sample and reports the resulting *ratings.*

noise level Trade jargon for *advertising weight level.*

off-the-card A term applied to advertising purchased at rates lower than the published rates. Most advertising is negotiated and purchased off-the-card. See also **rate card.**

open rate The highest rate charged for magazine or newspaper space. Does not include earned volume discounts or frequency discounts.

opt in (e-mail) An e-mail sales model in which potential consumers of a product or service are not sent sales-oriented e-mail unless they request it. See also **opt out.**

optimizers Mathematical formulas designed to provide either maximum reach or maximum frequency for a given budget in a given market or market group.

opt out (e-mail) An e-mail sales model in which potential consumers of a product or service are offered sales-oriented e-mail that will be sent unless they specifically ask that it *not* be sent to them. See also **opt in.**

outdoor Display advertising posted, painted, or erected outside. These messages may appear on boards, walls, support platforms, and so on.

out-of-home Sometimes used as a synonym for *outdoor.* But out-of-home also includes other advertising such as transit displays, bus cards, taxi posters, fully decorated buses, skywriting, sports stadium boards, and so on.

package A group of TV or radio programs or commercial spots offered (usually at a discount) by a station or network.

pass along reader A person who is not a subscriber or newsstand purchaser of a periodical but who reads a copy purchased or subscribed to by someone else. This readership count is monitored by various auditing companies.

payment-in-kind Products and services used to satisfy some or all of an invoice for sponsorship benefits.

penetration The degree, usually expressed as a percentage, to which a medium or vehicle has achieved coverage of a particular target market.

piggyback Back-to-back scheduling of two or more product or service commercials for a single company or brand. Essentially allows the advertiser to schedule two fifteen-second commercials for different products for the cost of a thirty-second commercial for a single product.

pod A group of commercials running in the hour, quarter-hour, half-hour and three-quarters-of-an-hour positions.

position (1) The location of a print advertisement in a periodical. (2) The location of a commercial on TV or radio with respect to the programming.

PRIZM A system of geodemographic segmentation for targeting specific portions of the U.S. adult population. Using U.S. Department of Census data, PRIZM classifies each neighborhood unit across the country into one of forty defined target clusters, on the theory that individuals who are demographically similar will live in geographical proximity.

product protection A guarantee to separate ads or commercials of competing companies or brands by some specific minimum time.

property An organization, event, or celebrity that is sponsorable.

proof of performance A report detailing the benefits delivered to the sponsor. See also **affidavit.**

psychographics Characteristics attributed to an individual (or group of individuals) and reflecting lifestyle, attitudes, and personality.

rating point The basic unit of measurement of audience size. One rating point equals 1 percent of the total potential audience (households or individuals).

rate card A published listing of charges for advertising units for any medium.

rate protection A guarantee given to an advertiser that rates will not be raised for some specified period of time. Often used to encourage additional advertising with a particular medium.

reach The total number of different homes or individuals exposed to an advertisement or commercial (exposure does not imply that an individual has necessarily seen, read, or understood the message). Reach is usually (but not always) expressed as the percentage of the total population or population target exposed over a given time period.

reach and frequency curve A curve showing the distribution of frequency in relation to the target reached over a given period of time (typically a campaign interval). It provides a graphic answer to the question, "How many people have seen [or heard or read] our message once? twice? three times? [and so on]?"

readership The total audience of a print vehicle. Calculated by multiplying circulation by readers per copy.

recency A description of the proximity of an advertising exposure to the time of purchase. It is used in relation to a theory proposing that for many types of advertising, the most effective frequency level is one exposure at an appropriate time rather than the more traditionally accepted three (or more) exposures.

remnant space Unsold magazine, outdoor, or other advertising space that cannot be "hidden" by the medium. Such space typically becomes available when an advertiser drops out of a contractual outdoor placement, print media insertion, or TV or radio time commitment at the last moment. Remnant space is typically sold at a significant discount, and often "reserved" for long-term, loyal direct response advertisers.

retail rates Rates for local retail advertisers. Newspaper retail rates are traditionally lower than national rates.

ROP Abbreviation for *run-of-press,* a description of an item such as an advertisement that an editor can insert anywhere in a newspaper because a particular position has not been requested.

ROS Abbreviation for *run-of-station,* a description of a broadcast commercial or announcement for which no particular time period has been requested and that the station can run at any time between 6:00 A.M. and 2:00 A.M. ROS spots are usually sold at a special low rate.

rotation The placements and times agreed on by an advertiser and a TV or radio station for commercials to run during the broadcast day or week.

saturation Simultaneous achievement of near maximum coverage and high levels of frequency by a specific medium or mix of media.

Scarborough A comprehensive media/market study of DMAs that collects a broad range of data, including demographic characteristics, newspaper and other print media usage, radio and TV use, product usage, and shopping habits from a group of respondents.

scatter market The network TV commercial market remaining after the major network advertisers and program sponsors have contracted with the networks for the broadcast year. This commercial time is purchased quarterly.

share-of-audience The percentage of all households using television (HUT) tuned to a particular station or cable channel. Also referred to simply as *share*.

share-of-market (SOM) Sales of a company's product or service as a percentage of the total sales (regional or national) in the product or service class.

share-of-voice An advertiser's share of gross rating points (GRPs) in a specific advertising category and a specific market area, expressed as a percentage of the total GRPs.

shelf talker Small signs placed at the point of sale in retail, most commonly on shelves in grocery aisles to attract the eye and convey a promotional message.

short rate The rate charged an advertiser when a frequency discount or volume discount rate contract is not completed and the discount therefore, is not earned, resulting in an additional cost to the advertiser.

showing Audience exposure to signage or outdoor advertising, calculated as a percentage although the term *percent* is often not used. "A 100 showing," for example, sometimes referred to as a *full showing*, means 100 percent coverage of the market. The number of outdoor signs required for a full showing differs from market to market.

Simmons Short form of *SMRB* or *Simmons Market Research Bureau, a* research organization measuring media audience characteristics, especially for magazines, and cross-referencing audience data with product usage data.

simulcast To broadcast a radio program on two stations at the same time (typically, "sister" AM and FM stations) or a TV program and a radio program with the TV program audio at the same time.

skew A shift, to left or right, of any distribution curve. Typically used to describe the amount by which any medium's audience deviates from the normal distribution curve for a given demographic.

SMSA Abbreviation for *standard metropolitan statistical area.* Major metropolitan areas, usually smaller than DMAs, are defined by the federal government.

sponsorship A marketing strategy that requires an investment of cash, goods, or services to gain access to the marketing assets of a sponsorable property to promote or otherwise position the sponsor in the marketplace.

sponsor A person or entity that exchanges cash or in-kind goods and services for access to specific rights and benefits of a property for commercial purposes.

sponsee The beneficiary of a sponsor's investment, the property.

spot A radio or TV commercial, 15, 30, 60, or 120 seconds in length.

spot TV Television time offered by local TV stations, both network affiliates and independents.

SRDS Abbeviation for *Standard Rate And Data Service*, an organization publishing advertising rates, circulation data, and mechanical requirements for periodicals of all types, spot TV, radio, outdoor advertising, and the Web.

strategic philanthropy The objective of corporate foundation giving programs aimed at improving the company's reputation, profile, and relationship with its customers.

sweep periods Survey periods during which local audience levels are measured for TV and radio. Also called *sweeps weeks* or often simply *sweeps*.

syndication The process of selling TV or radio programs (or bartered) to individual stations for airing over a given period of time. Some *syndicated programs* are reruns of programs first aired on a network; others are original programming. The sellers and distributors are called *syndicators*.

target audience A population segment identified as the most appropriate audience for a particular advertising campaign. That is, the audience the marketer has determined uses, or is most likely to use, the brand, product, or service offered. See also **demographics, psychographics.**

target rating points (TRPs) Accumulated ratings for a specific demographic target. Calculated by multiplying reach for that target by frequency. See also **gross rating points.**

tearsheet A page of advertising matter torn from the pages of a publication as a proof that the advertising was published according to contractual agreement.

telemarketing Use of the telephone to contact a potential customer.

test market Any marketing area (typically a DMA or SMSA) chosen to test a new product or service, and the advertising and other marketing support efforts for that product or service.

title sponsor A premium benefit that incorporates the sponsoring company's name in the title of the event, for example, the Buick Classic Golf Tournament, the Billabong World Surfing Championship, Sear's Theatre Fever Festival.

trade magazine A magazine edited and distributed to specific members of a limited and defined occupational group. As a group, also called *the trades* or *trade books.*

trade Payment-in-kind for advertising space or time.

traffic The function of getting commercials to stations, ad materials to print media, and so on. Also called *trafficking.*

traffic patterns Measurements of automotive or other consumer traffic flow and volume. Used to evaluate the suitability of outdoor boards or transit advertising for a specific marketing task.

transit advertising Posters or other forms of advertising appearing on buses, bus stop shelters, subways, commuter trains, airport hallways, and other transportation venues.

UHF Abbreviation for *ultra-high frequency,* the broadcast TV band on which channels 14 through 83 are aired.

unduplicated reach The portion of readership, viewership, or listenership that is unique to particular media vehicle. These people receive *only* that vehicle as an information source for the advertising message being delivered.

unwired network TV or radio stations not otherwise affiliated with each other that are all selected by an advertiser to deliver an advertising message.

Valpak Short for Valpak Direct Marketing Systems, a service mailing advertising (typically couponed advertising) to specific zip codes.

VALS A system of categorizing individuals into groups according to psychographic characteristics, and positioning those groups according to geographical location.

value-added promotion A promotion whose cost is subsumed in the advertiser's media buy. Small additional costs may be incurred, but the typical value-added promotion is "free" to the participating advertiser. Radio remotes are a common type of value-added promotion offered to advertisers. Many other types exist.

vehicle An individual advertising medium such as a magazine, a TV station, and so on.

vertical rotation The distribution of broadcast spots at different times over a single broadcast day.

visit Access a homepage or other URL location. A visit is sometimes called a *hit*.

VPVH Abbreviation for *viewers per viewing household*. Calculated by dividing the number of viewing individuals in a specific demographic group by the number of viewing households (sets in use).

voice The sum total of all gross rating points, for both print and electronic impressions, in a specific advertising category, geographical area, and time period.

volume discount A discount for buying a large amount of advertising pages, newspaper linage, or commercial time.

waste circulation Advertisement readership, viewership, or listenership that is outside the advertiser's target demographic group or geographical trading area.

Web Abbreviation for *World Wide Web*.

Web browser A software program with a graphical interface allowing a user to navigate from place to place on the Web by clicking on a key word or graphic.

Webcast (1) Use of e-mail as a selling tool on the Web (this meaning is not currently used much). (2) *Radio on the Web*, playing over loudspeakers hooked to a computer's sound card. (3) *TV on the Web*, with streaming video (live or taped), streaming audio, and sometimes other Web features such as chat space, advertising, and so on, surrounding the visual elements of the Webcast. Webcasting may be used internally to educate or train people or to introduce products to sales personnel or externally for *infomercials* to consumers. The ability to receive a Webcast is dependent on user hardware and the data capacity of the user's Internet access method.

Web site A homepage, and any additional pages layered behind that homepage, on the Web.

References

Clark, K., and Fujimoto, T. "The Power of Product Integrity." *Harvard Business Review,* Nov.–Dec. 1990, pp. 107–118.

Durgee, J. F., O'Connor, G. C., and Veryzer, R. W. "Observations: Training Values into Product Wants." *Journal of Advertising Research,* 1996, 36(6), 90–99.

Eagan, D. *Response to LitLamp Sponsor Survey.* Deerfield, Ill.: LitLamp Communications Group, Jan. 2002.

Griffin, B. Interview by the author. Seattle, Wash., Oct. 12, 2002.

Halpern, M. Interview by the author. Chicago, Jan. 2002.

Hamburg, S. "Myths About Relationships That Endure." Presentation at Wilmette Community House, Wilmette, Ill., Apr. 27, 2002.

Hayward, B. Member of Wheels in Motion cycling club. Interview by the author. Brighton, Mich., July 14, 2002.

"Interview with Watts Wacker." *Brandweek,* Apr. 14, 1997, p. 28.

Kawasaki, G., with Mareno, M. *Rules for Revolutionaries: The Capitalist Manifesto for Creating and Marketing New Products and Services.* New York: HarperBusiness, 1999.

Keating, A. Interview by the author. New York, Sept. 19, 2002.

Knapp, C. Interview by the author. Chicago, Aug. 5, 2002.

LaRouche, J. Interview by the author. Chicago., Sept. 2002.

Lyga, B. Interview by the author. Timonium, Md., May 1, 2003.

McCullough, L. *Response to LitLamp Sponsor Survey.* Washington, D.C.: LitLamp Communications Group, Jan. 2002.

Passmore, C. F. Interview by the author. Bethesda, Md., May 2, 2003.

Quester, P., and Thompson, B. "Advertising and Promotion Leverage on Arts Sponsorship Effectiveness." *Journal of Advertising,* Jan.–Feb. 2001, pp. 33–47.

Reed, M. H. *IEG Legal Guide to Sponsorship.* Chicago: IEG, 1989.

Reitelman, S. Interview by the author. Detroit, Mar. 7, 2002.

Renwall, C. Interview by the author. Palatine, Ill., Sept. 10, 2002.

Retherford, W. Interview by the author. Chicago, May 20, 2000.

Salerno, M. B. Interview by the author. New York, Oct. 11, 2002.

Sjodin, T. *New Sales Speak.* New York: Wiley, 2001.

Woods, L. "Tax Treatment of Corporate Sponsorship Payments to Exempt Organizations." *Journal of Taxation,* Sept. 2002, pp. 174–182.

Index

A

Advertising agencies, 67–68

Advertising fees, subject to UBIT, 90–91

American Library Association, proposal cover, 56

Apparel companies, as potential sponsors, 25

Apple Computer, product placement in motion pictures, 11

Aspiration, as value brought to sponsors, 9

Assessment: of assets nonprofits offer sponsors, 26–30; of audience, 15–17; of cultural readiness for sponsorship, 12–13, 19–20; of sponsor market, 22–25; of value of intangible assets, 39–43

Assets: exchange of, for fees, 19, 31; important to sponsors, 6–12; intangible, assessing value of, 39–43; marketing plans built on, 32–37; media, 29; nonprofit's audience as, 15–18; worksheets for determining, 26–29

Attorneys: for drafting sponsorship agreements, 94; final deals reviewed by, 84–85; for help in avoiding UBIT, 92

Attracting sponsors. *See* Selling sponsorships

Audience: assessing, 15–17; importance of knowledge of, 20; information in proposals on, 52–53, 57, 60; market research on, 18, 27; people of interest to sponsors in, 15–17; targeted, as value brought to sponsors, 10

Authenticity, as value brought to sponsors, 6–7

Automotive companies, as potential sponsors, 25

B

Banks, as potential sponsors, 23–24

Bartering media, 82

Beverage companies, as potential sponsors, 23

Bloomingdale's: media clips as selling point for, 61; as partner in *Hairspray*, 17

Board members, obtaining sponsorships with help from, 67

Bounce-back tracking, 107

Brand visibility, offered to sponsors, 53

Brooklyn Academy of Music (BAM), quality programming emphasized by, 19

Bumbershoot Art Festival (Seattle), description of sponsorship property, 56

Business channels, 15–16

Business ventures, sponsorships as, 3–5, 19–20, 31, 53–54

Businesses, identifying, as potential sponsors, 22–25

Businesspeople: as audience members of interest to sponsors, 15; importance of regular contact with, 20

C

Cause marketing: caution on caps in, 80; defined, xv; value brought to sponsor by, 8–9

Ceres Collegiate Foundation, women's cardiac care initiative, 34–37

Chicago Children's Hospital, sponsor seminar hosted by, 64

Chicago Highland Games, media attention for, 17

Chicago Software Association, Sponsorship Bootcamp hosted by, 39

Children's Miracle Network, cause marketing with retailer chains by, 10

Civic leaders, as audience members of interest to sponsors, 17

Clark, K., 7

Closing the deal, when selling sponsorships, 82–83

Coaching, by corporate foundation officers, 65

Coca Cola, school activities sponsored by, 12, 17

Cold calling, 72–74

Commitment: long-term, to sponsorships, 113; as value brought to sponsors, 6

Communications, with sponsors, 108–109

Competitors, pricing by, 37–39, 40

Consumer values, as asset brought to sponsors, 8–9

Convention activity fees, taxation of, 91

Corporate foundations, 65–67

Corporate headquarters, as potential sponsor, 22–23

Corporate relations committee, 21

Cost per thousand (CPM), 45
Costs: defining, when negotiating with sponsors, 81; implementation, 44–45; media, as pricing consideration, 45; pricing based on, vs. promotional value, 5
Culture: clash between nonprofit and sponsor, 109–110; of nonprofits ready for sponsorships, 12–13, 19

D

Database usage fees, taxation of, 91
Databases: caution on releasing, to mailing houses, 81; created through sponsorship events, 107
Deal flow, 70–71
Deals, defined, xv
Decision makers: cold calling, 73; handling objections by, 75–76; help for, given to sponsors in proposals, 51–54; meetings with, 74–78; negotiating with, 78–82
DePaul University, timetable for Centennial Campaign, 68, 69
Diamond Comic Book Distributors, lifestyle research by, 15
Distributors, as audience members of interest to sponsors, 16
Durgee, J. F., 8

E

Eagan, D., 72
Efficiency, as value brought to sponsors, 10
Emotional experience, as value brought to sponsors, 7–8
End-users, as audience members of interest to sponsors, 15
Endorsements: and morals clauses, 95, 98; taxation of fees for, 91
Envelopes, mailing, for proposal kits, 54
Exchange, 19, 31
Exclusivity fees, taxation of, 89–90, 92
Exit surveys, 107

F

Fact sheets, in proposals, 57, 59
Fees: exchange of assets for, 19, 31; and force majeure clauses, 98, 110; UBIT regulations applied to, 88–91
Final reports, on sponsorships, 111–112
Financial services companies, as potential sponsors, 23–24
Force majeure clauses, in sponsorship agreements, 98, 110
Fujimoto, T., 7

G

Goals, sales, 20
Griffin, B., 4
Guaranteed exposure fees, taxation of, 91

H

Hairspray, Bloomingdale's as partner in production of, 17
Halpern, M., 20
Hamburg, S., 6

Harley Davidson, Muscular Dystrophy Association sponsorship by, 8–9
Hayward, B., 7
Hybrid deals, defined, xv
Hyperlinks to sponsor's Web site, UBIT exemption for, 89

I

IBM, Olympics sponsorship by, 11
IEG Sponsorship Report newsletter, 39
Illinois St. Andrew Society, Chicago Highland Games hosted by, 17
Implementation costs, 44–45
In-kind contributions, 81
Industry regulators, as audience members of interest to sponsors, 17
Insights, as value brought to sponsors, 11
Insubstantial value, and UBIT laws, 87–88
Intangible assets: assessing value of, 39–43; important to sponsors, 6–9. *See also* Assets
Interaction, as value brought to sponsors, 7
International Events Group, *IEG Sponsorship Report* newsletter, 39

J

Janus, M., 3–4

K

Kawasaki, G., 54
Keating, A., 17, 61
Knapp, C., 6

L

LaRouche, J., 16
Lawyers. *See* Attorneys
League of Chicago Theatres, aggressive promotion by, 20
Lifestyle validation, as value brought to sponsors, 6
Logos, sponsor, UBIT exemption for use of, 88–89, 92
Lyga, B., 15

M

Mailing lists: caution on releasing, 81; created through sponsorship events, 107
Market research, on audience, 18, 27
Marketing agencies, 109–110
Marketing plans: benefits of, 32; creating, 33–34; sample, 34–37; using existing, 32–33
Marks, sponsor, UBIT exemption for use of, 88–89
McCullough, L., 61
Measurement: of media efficiency, 45; methods for, when implementing sponsorship program, 102, 107; of nonprofit's audience, 18, 27
Media: assets related to, 29; as audience of interest to sponsors, 16–17; bartering prepurchased, 82; calculating value of, 45; clips from, 60–61, 64. *See also* Public relations
Media companies, as potential sponsors, 23
Media strategies, 32, 37

Meetings with sponsors: first, 74–76; getting first, 72–74; to implement sponsorship agreement, 101; rejection/success ratios in arranging, 74; second, 76–78; worksheet for taking minutes at, 101

Memorandum of intent, 94, 95

Mercedes-Benz, COMDEX Tech Talks sponsored by, 9

Miller, M., 37–38

Minutes, worksheet for taking, 101

Morals clauses, in sponsorship agreements, 95, 98

Motion pictures, product placement in, 11

Motivation of retailers, as value brought to sponsors, 10–11

Ms. Foundation for Women, *Seventeen* magazine sponsorship of, 11

MTV, and Rock the Vote campaign, 53

Muscular Dystrophy Association, Harley Davidson sponsorship of, 8–9

Museum of Contemporary Art (Chicago), First Friday events, xiii

Museum of Modern Art, slogan, 57

N

NASCAR: and breakfast cereal brands sponsoring stock cars, 10; sponsorship selling by, 72

National Breast Cancer Prevention Organization, sample offer letter, 55

National Park Service, Proud Partners of America's National Parks sponsorship program, 108–109

National PTA, excerpts from proposal for, 52–53, 57

Negotiating with sponsors, 78–82. *See also* Selling sponsorships

New York Library Association's Summer Reading Program, Wegmans food chain's sponsorship of, 10–11

Nissan X-Terra sport utility vehicles, triathlon sponsored by, 7

Noncompete clauses, in sponsorship agreements, 98

Nonprofits: change in thinking in, necessary for sponsorships, 3–5; culture of sponsor vs. culture of, 109–110; with culture ready for sponsorships, 19–20; determining sponsorship readiness of, 12–13; gauging newsworthiness of, 17

O

O'Connor, G. C., 8

Offer letters, 54, 55

Olympics: IBM's sponsorship of, 11; Visa's sponsorship of, 108; Winter, Sara Lee's action to catch media attention at, 16–17

On-site sales, opportunity for, as value brought to sponsors, 12

P

Passmore, C., 108

Pepsi, school activities sponsored by, 12, 17

Policies. *See* Sponsorship policies

Prazmark, R., 94

Press books, 64

Pricing sponsorships, 31–47; and assessing value of intangible assets, 39–43; based on cost vs. promotional value, 5; comparative analysis of, 37–39, 40; example of, 47; factors determining, 31, 44; and implementation costs, 44–45; and media costs, 45; overview of, 31–32; worksheet for calculating, 46

Product display, UBIT exemption for, 89

Product placement, in motion pictures, 11

Product trials, 107

Products, opportunity to showcase, as value brought to sponsors, 11

Program theft, 98

Property, defined, xiv

Proposal kits, 54–62; mailing envelopes for, 54; offer letters in, 54–55; proposal components in, 56–61; proposal cover sheets in, 56; response devices in, 62

Proposals, 51–62; audience information in, 52–53, 57, 60; body of, 56–57, 58; caution on attaching sponsorship agreement to, 94; decision-making help for sponsors in, 51–54; fact sheets in, 57, 59; media clips in, 60–61; purposes of, 51, 62; summary of rights and benefits in, 61; testimonials from previous sponsors in, 60; title pages for, 56. *See also* Proposal kits

Public relations: drawing sponsor attention to nonprofits through, 64–65; strategies for, 32; as value brought to sponsors, 9. *See also* Media

Q

Quaker Oats, SeniorNet sponsorship by, 11

Qualified sponsorship payments (QSPs), and UBIT laws, 87, 92

Quester, P., 65

Questions: addressed by sponsorship policies, 21; to determine nonprofits' readiness for sponsorships, 12–13

R

Ravinia Music Festival, liquor distributor partnership in, 16

Record keeping: to satisfy UBIT regulations, 66, 90, 92; for sponsorship deals with corporate foundations, 66

Reed, M. H., 98

Reitelman, S., 19

Renewals of sponsorships, 112–113

Renwall, C., 39

Reports, final, on sponsorships, 111–112

Research: market, on audience, 18, 27; on pricing by competitors, 37–39

Response devices, in proposal kits, 62

Retail companies, as potential sponsors, 10–11, 24–25

Retherford, W., 17

Rock the Vote campaign, and MTV, 53

Royalty payments, UBIT exemption for, 89

S

Salerno, M. B., 66, 77

Sales: defined, xv; goals for, 20; on-site, opportunity for, as value brought to sponsors, 12

Sales receipts, 107

Sampling, UBIT exemption for, 89

Sampling distribution, 107

San Francisco Jazz Fest, slogan, 57

Sara Lee, attracted media attention at Winter Olympics, 16–17

Selling points, in proposals, 56–57, 58

Selling sponsorships, 63–85; to advertising agencies, 67–68; balancing work and personal life when, 85; board member assistance with, 67; closing the deal when, 82–83; cold calling for, 72–74; to corporate foundations, 65–67; deal flow for, 70–71; in meetings with sponsors, 74–78; negotiation process for, 78–82; public relations efforts for, 64–65; reviewing final deal when, 84–85; sponsorship seminars for, 63–64; suggested activities during delays when, 83; timetable for, 68, 69

SeniorNet, Quaker Oats sponsorship of, 11

Seventeen magazine, Ms. Foundation for Women sponsorship by, 11

Sjodin, T., 82

Slogans, sponsor: selling points expressed in, 57; UBIT exemption for use of, 88–89, 92

Sponsees, defined, xv

Sponsor market, assessment of, 22–25

Sponsors: advocating for, 102; arranging networking by, 63–64; cold calling, 72–74; communications with, 108–109; culture of nonprofits vs. culture of, 109–110; decision-making help for, in proposals, 51–54; defined, xv; defining categories of, 81; dissatisfied, 110–111; identifying potential, 22–25; negotiating with, 78–82; offering visibility for brands of, 53; testimonials from previous, in proposals, 60; types of people in audience of interest to, 15–17; values nonprofits can offer to, 6–12; withholding information, 79–80. *See also* Meetings with sponsors

Sponsorship agreements: benefits of, 93; caution on attaching to proposals, 94; force majeure clauses in, 98, 110; implementing, 100–108; memo of intent as substitute for, 94, 95; morals clauses in, 95, 98; noncompete clauses in, 98; template for, 94, 96–97; tips on drafting, 93–94; value of sponsor benefits in, 93

Sponsorship policies: creating, 20–21; sample, 22

Sponsorship proposals. *See* Proposals

Sponsorship seminars, 63–64

Sponsorships: as business ventures, 3–5, 19–20, 53–54; change in thinking required for, 3–5; culture of nonprofits ready for, 19–20; defined, xiv; final reports on, 111–112; history of, xi–xii; long-term commitment to, 113; questions to determine nonprofits' readiness for, 12–13; renewals of, 112–113; values nonprofits offer in, 6–12. *See also* Pricing sponsorships; Selling sponsorships

St. Patrick's Block Party (Chicago), slogan, 57

Staff: listing responsibilities of, 102, 103–106; ready to work with sponsors, 30

Strategic philanthropy, defined, xv

Substantial return benefits, and UBIT laws, 87, 92

Summary of rights and benefits, in proposals, 61

Sundance Film Festival, slogan, 57

Swap outs, 82

Sweepstakes, 107

T

Tangible assets: important to sponsors, 9–12; marketing plans built on, 32–37. *See also* Assets

Tax issues. *See* Unrelated business income tax (UBIT) regulations

Telecommunications companies, as potential sponsors, 24

Testimonials from previous sponsors, in proposals, 60

Thompson, B., 65

Timetable, for selling sponsorships, 68, 69

Trade show activity fees, taxation of, 91

Trademarks, sponsor, UBIT exemption for use of, 88–89

U

Unrelated business income tax (UBIT) regulations: guidelines on, 91–93; insubstantial value and, 87–88; qualified sponsorship payments (QSPs) and, 87, 92; record keeping to satisfy, 66, 90, 92; sponsor benefits exempt from, 86, 88–89; sponsor benefits subject to, 86, 89–91; and sponsorship agreements attached to proposals, 94; substantial return benefits and, 87, 92

U.S. Congress members, as audience of interest to sponsors, 17

V

Value: of in-kind payments, 81; insubstantial, and UBIT laws, 87–88; of intangible assets, 39–43; promotional, to sponsor, 5; of sponsor benefits, and sponsorship agreements, 93

Values: consumer, 8–9; personal, 8, 44. *See also* Assets

Veryzer, R. W., 8

Visa, Olympics sponsorship by, 108

Visibility, as value brought to sponsors, 9

W

Wacker, W., 6

Web sites, sponsor, UBIT exemption for hyperlinks to, 89

Wegmans food chain, sponsorship of New York Library Association's Summer Reading Program, 10–11

Woods, L., 87, 88, 92–93

Written agreements. *See* Sponsorship agreements

Written policies. *See* Sponsorship policies